QUANTUM CARE

QUANTUM CARE

A Deep Dive into AI for
Health Delivery and Research

ROHIT MAHAJAN

Advantage | Books

Published by Advantage, Charleston, South Carolina.
Member of Advantage Media.

ADVANTAGE is a registered trademark, and the Advantage colophon is a trademark of Advantage Media Group, Inc.

Printed in the United States of America.

10 9 8 7 6 5 4 3 2 1

ISBN: 978-1-64225-554-6 (Paperback)
ISBN: 978-1-64225-553-9 (eBook)

LCCN: 2022923131

Cover design by Jivan Davé.
Layout design by David Taylor.

This publication is designed to provide accurate and authoritative information in regard to the subject matter covered. It is sold with the understanding that the publisher is not engaged in rendering legal, accounting, or other professional services. If legal advice or other expert assistance is required, the services of a competent professional person should be sought.

Advantage Media helps busy entrepreneurs, CEOs, and leaders write and publish a book to grow their business and become the authority in their field. Advantage authors comprise an exclusive community of industry professionals, idea-makers, and thought leaders. Do you have a book idea or manuscript for consideration? We would love to hear from you at **AdvantageMedia.com**.

*In memory of my father. His journey as a patient inspired
me to make a difference in healthcare.*

CONTENTS

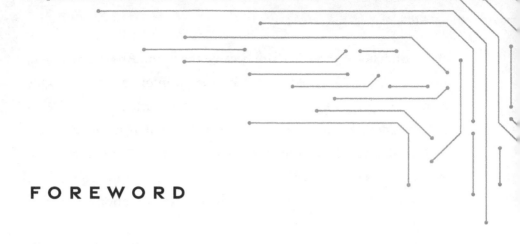

FOREWORD

In the summer of 2019, I met Dr. Tomislav (Tom) Mihaljevic, the CEO of Cleveland Clinic. I had known Tom since 2013, when he attended the General Management program that I chaired at the Harvard Business School. Tom was familiar with my work on digital transformation, and he asked me to help him and his team to create a blueprint for Cleveland Clinic's digital journey. Although I had been doing work in the digital strategy area for more than a decade and even wrote a book on this topic, *Driving Digital Strategy*, I did not have a deep knowledge of the healthcare industry. Working with Tom and his senior leadership team gave me the front-row seat to understand the enormous potential of digital technology in the healthcare sector. I had many discussions with Tom and his senior leadership team, as well as several meetings with leaders from Google and Microsoft, to map out potential directions for Cleveland Clinic's digital strategy. We explored how Cleveland Clinic could use technology to digitize its current operations, leverage data to get new insights, and embark on new opportunities enabled by technology.

In March 2020, the pandemic upended our lives, and digital transformation in the healthcare industry went into an overdrive.

Work from home and telehealth became the norm. Around this time, Rohit Mahajan contacted me to become an informal advisor to his company BigRio. I knew Rohit from the time he attended our Owner and President Management Program (OPM) at Harvard Business School. Rohit and I kept in touch since then, and after becoming an advisor to his company, I came to know more about his expertise in data and technology. During our numerous conversations, I learned many things from his experience.

Rohit is an experienced entrepreneur and leader in the technology and software industries. For several decades, he has provided innovative data and analytical solutions to his clients in several industries including healthcare, automotive, financial services, retail, and manufacturing. I am thrilled that he has decided to distill his expertise and experience in this book with a focus on healthcare.

In this book, Rohit covers a vast range of technologies—artificial intelligence (AI), cognitive digital twins (CDT), Internet of Things (IoT), and many others—and their impact on the healthcare industry. For example, using data from a patient's electronic health record, Google researchers have developed AI models that can predict the course of a disease for the patient and the risk of death during a hospital stay with 95 percent accuracy. Using massive amounts of data and AI, Moderna was able to develop a new vaccine for COVID-19 in months that would have otherwise taken years. In the process, Moderna developed an mRNA platform that can be easily tweaked to develop new vaccines quickly.

Cognitive digital twin (CDT), or a virtual replica of a physical system, can gather data from real objects through sensors and run simulations to predict potential failures and suggest possible improvements. This approach has been used in the manufacturing industry for several years, and there is good reason to believe that it can be a powerful way to model, monitor, and improve the operations of medical devices such as a pacemaker or a surgical implant, and even the human body. Siemens and Philips are working on versions of a virtual heart using AI and CDT technology.

These CDT systems are powered by IoT devices that have built-in sensors to monitor the performance of a device or organ. Companies like Becton Dickinson and Abbott are creating connected devices with built-in chips and sensors that provide real-time data about a patient's health condition.

Emergence of these technologies and their potential impact on healthcare has also created a lot of excitement among entrepreneurs and venture capitalists. Livingo, a start-up that focused on helping patients manage diabetes by monitoring their blood glucose levels, was sold to Teledco in 2020, for $18.5 billion. Many other unicorns have been born in the last decade that have focused on leveraging technology to manage healthcare.

Innovative technologies have already made significant impact in the healthcare industry, and even bigger shifts are yet to come. Rohit paints a clear picture that allows readers to understand these innovative technologies and their future directions. Based on his practical experience, he also highlights implementation challenges that senior executives must navigate to realize the full potential of these innovations.

I enjoyed reading this book and gained a deeper appreciation of how technology will shape the future of healthcare.

SUNIL GUPTA

Edward W. Carter Professor of Business,
Harvard Business School

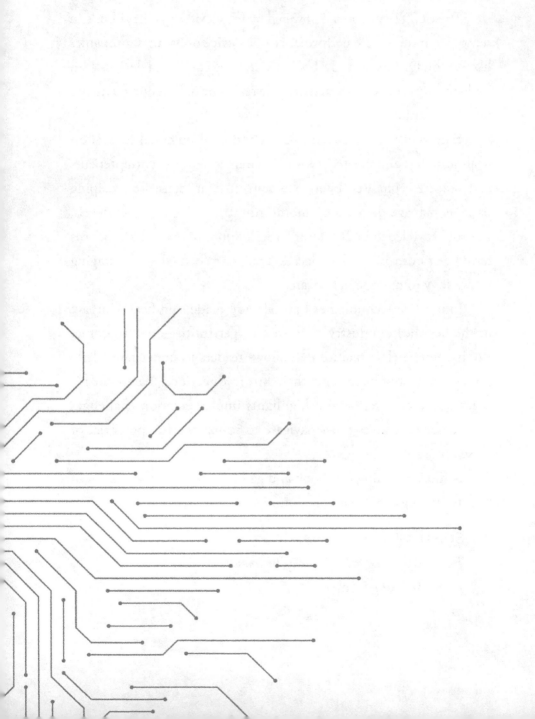

INTRODUCTION

Can Machines Think?

Some people call this artificial intelligence, but the reality is this technology will enhance us. So instead of artificial intelligence, I think we'll augment our intelligence.

—GINNI ROMETTY

According to *The AI Index 2021 Annual Report*, created by Stanford University, "AI systems can now compose text, audio, and images to a sufficiently high standard that humans have a hard time telling the difference between synthetic and non-synthetic outputs for some constrained applications of the technology."

Think about that for a moment.

That means that we are at a point in the development of artificial intelligence where, at many touchpoints with AI, we cannot tell if we are interacting with humans or computers.

I suppose that I knew that this is where artificial intelligence could go when I wrote my first AI program in 1988. But even I did not imagine we would get to this point so quickly, or what the implications could be for AI and machine learning in general, and more specifically, for improving the delivery of healthcare.

The Early Days

I think I became fascinated with the idea of artificial intelligence quite early on. I was always interested in new technology. As I was advancing in my studies in computer science, I knew that people had been working on AI for quite some time, but when I was in engineering school in 1988, it was not really part of the curriculum that our professors were teaching. However, there was a group of friends and I who were really drawn to AI and intrigued by its possibilities. We all agreed that this was why we got into computing in the first place. AI was not simple programming or process automation; this really had the ability to change the world.

We developed a voracious appetite for AI and started reading all the material we could on the subject until we could write our own AI programs. Coincidentally, the first one I wrote in 1988 had to do with healthcare. I guess, even then—on some level, either conscious or subconscious—I knew that was where AI could make a major contribution to society.

I was doing an internship at a big corporate tech company in India, and I wound up writing this program that when you input the symptoms on one side, it would predict the disease or condition on the other. Predictions based on data sets are the cornerstone of AI.

Now, of course, an AI program that can predict disease based on a set of symptoms is already being used quite extensively today. But then, it was just kind of a vanity starter project during my internship. The other tools we have now that make that kind of AI in medicine a practical reality simply were not available. I never really went anywhere with it and continued to watch advancements in AI from the sidelines.

I did get into the industry, however, and worked with top companies like IBM, but not in AI development. Yet, it always remained in the back of my mind, like a slowly developing cocoon.

A Father's Journey

I lost my father to cancer.

It was his journey as a patient, I think, that brought my passion for how AI could radically change healthcare from a fly-like buzz in the back of my mind to something I had to do to change the world of medicine.

He had COPD and then later developed lung cancer. It was not pretty having to watch the progression of his disease up close. I knew if the AI programs I had toyed with in their infancies were available now, we could have had far more advanced diagnostics and screening tools that may have caught his disease earlier, before it had advanced to Stage Four, and things could have been quite different. It was that experience that really drove me to grab the opportunity with BigRio when it presented itself in 2019. And now, we have launched an AI studio specifically for U.S.-based healthcare start-ups, and we are partnering with start-ups developing healthcare solutions with AI at the core of their solutions.

In fact, one of those which I am personally working with specifically is a start-up that has developed an AI algorithm that can better predict lung cancer in COPD patients. While I can trace that one directly back to my family's experience, this is certainly a very wide canvas that stretches across almost every aspect of the healthcare industry. Indeed, right now, where we see the most activity in AI in healthcare is not so much on the clinical side but within the pharmaceutical segment in the area of drug discovery.

In fact, did you know that AI was instrumental in reducing the COVID-19 vaccine trials to months rather than years and in getting vaccines from the lab into people's arms to combat the deadly pandemic so quickly?

A Case in Point

Recently I had the pleasure of serving on a Harvard Business School case study panel with Stéphane Bancel, CEO of Moderna. AI and how it can be used to accelerate drug discovery was involved in how the Moderna COVID-19 vaccine was able to be developed so quickly, despite using very novel mRNA technology. The reason can be summed up by Bancel's own words that describe Moderna as "a tech company that happens to do biology."

I will get into this at greater length in later chapters in the book, but Moderna is the ideal real-world model of a company that utterly understands the power of AI and how it relates to biological sciences.

As Mr. Bancel so elegantly put it, he sees Moderna as a technology company that just happens to be involved in drug discovery. This means that at their core, they are set up more like a traditional tech company with all of the stacked technical devices and the knowledge and expertise, which includes AI and machine learning. Looking over the case study, I could immediately see that they have a thorough understanding of how to load huge amounts of data and how to deal with the integration of the data sources from the various different devices that they work with. From the time it reared its head in Wuhan to the time Moderna took on the task of antiviral development, there was a wealth of information available about the virus. Moderna's knowledge of how to leverage AI to process and make predictions very quickly on that volume of information allowed them to do in weeks what would have normally taken months or years.

It was their whole integrated approach to using AI from development to delivery that allowed them to roll past any other pharmaceutical company and deliver a vaccine in record time. Prior to this, the fastest vaccine to be developed and approved by the FDA was for the Mumps in 1967—it took four years! This, on its own, is a magnificent triumph for the global healthcare research community and for AI.

What is perhaps most significant about this achievement, though, is not only did AI help Moderna to deliver the vaccine in record time, it also was able very quickly to prove that a new approach to vaccines—mRNA technology—worked. And now it can be used as a kind of platform technology, like an iPhone, where it can be used to develop other vaccines and against other viruses, just like downloading different apps to your phone!

A Tribute and a Legacy

I do not think any of us ever could have imagined how the COVID-19 pandemic was going to be so devastating, particularly in my familial country of India. To me, there is no more fitting tribute or legacy to the memory of my father than the knowledge that the technology I am helping to develop and bring to the world was so instrumental in getting the lifesaving vaccines quickly yet safely to the public.

Right now, thanks to a convergence of many things—not the least of which is the success of the coronavirus vaccines—there are billions of dollars of investment going into AI for healthcare. If there is someone out there reading this book who has seen or maybe is seeing someone suffer the way I watched my father and is thinking, "I know a way to make this better," I want them to know if they are willing to take that leap of faith with me, money is available to support their vision.

AI in healthcare will fundamentally change how healthcare is delivered. It will improve patient outcomes, it will save lives, and it may very well be the greatest start-up and investment opportunity since the dot-com bubble of the 1980s.

AI in healthcare will fundamentally change how healthcare is delivered. It will improve patient outcomes, it will save lives, and it may very well be the greatest start-up and investment opportunity since the dot-com bubble of the 1980s.

PART I

The Trends

Genomics, artificial intelligence, and deep machine learning technologies are helping practitioners deliver better diagnosis and actually freeing up time for patient interaction.

—FRANS VAN HOUTEN

AI Today

I often tell my students not to be misled by the name "artificial intelligence"—there is nothing artificial about it. AI is made by humans, intended to behave by humans, and, ultimately, to impact humans' lives and human society.

—FEI-FEI LI

As we begin what will be a very deep dive into machine intelligence, let's start off by defining some terms that you will see in use throughout this book.

"AI," "deep learning," and "machine learning" are all the buzzwords you are hearing right now revolving around the field of artificial intelligence, especially in how AI is being used for business applications regarding analytics and Big Data.

Artificial intelligence (AI) and machine learning (ML) often get used interchangeably, but they are not exactly the same thing. At its most basic level, AI is a broad concept of machines being able to carry out tasks in a way that we would consider "smart." Machine learning takes that concept to the next level of machines that not only can perform smart tasks but can actually learn and then make decisions and predictions based on what they have learned.

Deep learning takes the AI concept to an even higher level. It is the cutting edge of the cutting edge, the space where machines not only learn but can be intuitive and come up with ideas on their own based on their extensive database of knowledge, learning, and "experience." In this sense, and how we will be discussing AI in this book, artificial intelligence is not just about intelligence but about intuition and insight, the kinds of cognitive abilities that we, until recently, only ascribed to the human mind. It is this aspect of where AI is today and where it is going that has the most profound applications—particularly in healthcare.

It was Alan Turing, the so-called "father of computer science," who first asked in 1950: "Can machines think?" To answer that question, he came up with the now well-known Turing Test, where a human interrogator would try to distinguish between a computer and a human text response. To this day, it remains an important part of the history of AI and has formed the basis of much of where we are with AI today, particularly around the introduction and ongoing advancements in linguistics and Natural Language Processing (NLP), which we will discuss at far greater length in our next chapter.

AI is our attempt to answer Turing's question in the affirmative. It is a far-reaching endeavor to replicate or simulate human intelligence in machines. However, it goes beyond that. AI, as we know it today, and its vast potential in general but particularly in healthcare, is not only about replicating human intelligence and intuition but augmenting it.

The Current Landscape of AI in Healthcare

We are already interacting with deep machine learning on a regular basis. Have you heard yourself or your friends ever ask the question, "How does Facebook, Google, Amazon, etc. show me ads for things that I was only just thinking about buying?" These large tech companies do not have hidden cameras in your homes or secret drones following you around. What they do have is advanced deep learning algorithms, and this is how Amazon gets to intuitively "decide" what you want to buy next, or Netflix "knows" what you want to watch.

At its core, AI is about learning by being able to interpret massive amounts of data and then, very quickly, being able to make extraordinarily accurate predictions based on the same. As you might imagine, that has some remarkable implications for the delivery of medicine and healthcare.

At its core, AI is about learning by being able to interpret massive amounts of data and then, very quickly, being able to make extraordinarily accurate predictions based on the same. As you might imagine, that has some remarkable implications for the delivery of medicine and healthcare.

Whether you know it or not, you already run into AI at various touchpoints in the healthcare system. One of the first practical applications of AI and healthcare is in the marriage between AI and medical devices, particularly imaging devices. If you think about diagnostic medical imaging, be it x-rays, CT scans, what have you, the images are taken of the body, and it is then up to the doctors and technicians to interpret those images and offer a diagnosis of what they could indicate. Machines using AI are much better at analyzing images down to the pixel level than the human eye could ever be. Combine that ability with instantaneous access to the entire database of medical images, and it is easy to see how AI has made medical imaging devices into astonishingly powerful tools.

It does not start and stop with smart medical devices. It is almost as if healthcare is the industry that was tailor-made for AI adoption. If you look across the entire healthcare landscape, basically, there are four stakeholders:

1. The providers—clinicians, hospitals, etc.

2. Pharmaceutical and biotech companies

3. Insurance companies

4. Patients and medical consumers

AI touches each of these stakeholders and benefits each of them in varied yet specific ways. Let us take a look at AI in healthcare today by looking at how it impacts each of the major stakeholders.

Benefits of AI to Healthcare Providers

Ultimately, for a hospital or other provider of healthcare, the biggest challenge faced is how to treat as many patients as you can, as safely and cost-effectively as possible. AI is the solution.

A company that we are familiar with provides an excellent example; it has to do with the neonatal intensive care unit or NICU. As you may know, the NICU in the hospital is an area that employs advanced technology and highly trained healthcare professionals to give special care to the tiniest and often the most fragile of patients.

The NICU leverages some of the highest value personal equipment and services in the facility. How do you allocate those resources correctly so that only the births that need that specialized care are using that specialized care, ensuring that NICU beds are available for the babies who need them the most?

This company developed an AI algorithm that could take vast amounts of data into account—medical history, lifestyle, family history, etc.—and very accurately screen out high-risk pregnancies from lower-risk pregnancies, and could provide a quite accurate prediction of the facility's patient population that might wind up needing the NICU. It also allowed practitioners to target those with potentially high-risk pregnancies and provide them with social workers, diet and lifestyle counselors, and other interventions that could keep them from winding up in need of NICU services. This system is being used by Johns Hopkins NICU right now. Johns Hopkins NICU has a Level IV designation from the American Academy of Pediatrics. That is the highest level available, so you can see why having a system in place to allocate their very specialized care is essential to public health.

Another example that is not so specific is hospitals that are using similar AI algorithms to lower their rates of people that regularly return to the emergency department for non-emergency care. This is a problem in all hospitals but in particular in low-income urban sectors, where people, because of lack of insurance or funds, use the emergency department for non-emergency care or wind up in the ER because they do not have the means to treat a condition when it is less serious. As in the case of the NICU, this again stretches the limited resources of the ER. AI is being used to help the administrators isolate their "frequent flyers" by predicting who they might be, and again, providing them with access to other clinical or social interventions, which can hopefully prevent a visit to the ER.

Because AI is so good at predicting medical outcomes, these are only a few examples of how it is serving as the cornerstone of what will be a new era of preventive medicine, where providers are able to be much more proactive and less reactive to the delivery of patient care.

Another area where AI is making a major difference on the provider side of healthcare is in making up for the dramatic short-falls in the labor force. Current estimates are that one-third of nurses currently serving the American public are baby boomers, who will retire by 2030, taking their knowledge with them. This drastic shortage in healthcare workers poses the imminent need for replacements. The problem of this shortage has only been made clearer and exacerbated by the COVID-19 crisis. The urgent need for additional clinical support is another area where AI can make a major difference.

Much like the examples where AI is being used to see who really needs critical care, such as the ICU or ER, it can be used to automate and streamline the processes for determining whether or not a patient actually needs to visit a doctor in-person or can benefit from a tele-medicine visit.

Many lower-level health-related questions and concerns could be addressed without a face-to-face consultation via mobile applications integrated with AI. These AI-powered applications can provide basic healthcare support by "bringing the doctor to the patient" and alleviating the need for the patient to leave the comfort of their home, let alone scheduling an appointment for an in-office visit to a doctor, thus saving time and resources for all parties involved. Should a patient need to see a doctor, these applications also contain schedulers capable of determining appointment type, length, urgency, and available dates/times, foregoing the need for constant human-based clinical support and interaction.

Benefits of AI to the Pharmaceutical Biotech Sector

As mentioned in the introduction, AI played a major role in fast-tracking the development of the COVID-19 vaccines. We will go into this in much greater length in a later chapter, but perhaps the area where AI is making the most dramatic impact on healthcare is in the drug development arena.

Drug development is a painstakingly lengthy procedure often involving years of research and clinical trial. AI can streamline this entire process.

Imagine you are a research scientist, and you could have direct and immediate access to every article written in every journal and the results of every clinical trial related to the topic you are researching? Just how much quicker would that speed up your own research? That is exactly what AI can do for drug discovery.

And it is not just the information that is in the published clinical papers. Any ordinary computer analysis could access that kind of information. AI can and does go much deeper. The truth is, particularly if you are researching something novel—like a new coronavirus—the vast majority of biomedical information is out there in unstructured formats that are in their raw form, such as doctor's notes, hospital admission records, coroner's reports, patent applications, and so on. AI, when coupled with Natural Language Processing (NLP) algorithms, offers a powerful solution to this problem. With NLP, AI algorithms are being written that can analyze any kind of documents and other datasets and identify biologically relevant text elements such as the names of genes, proteins, drugs, clinical manifestations of a particular disease, and anything else relevant to a given drug discovery team's target. That is only the starting point of AI and drug discovery.

We will get into this in greater detail later on, but the power of AI and drug discovery goes beyond merely being able to sift through and process vast amounts of data; it also has to do with the ability of AI to create 100 percent accurate virtual models, something that my friend and colleague, Dr. Ahmed El Adl refers to as a "cognitive digital twin." These cognitive digital twins can completely emulate complex systems—be that an aircraft or biomechanical systems such as a heart or a lung.

As I mentioned in the introduction, one of my collaborators, Dr. Himanshu Kaul, is currently exploring the development of a "virtual human lung" that can be used to test specific inhalers and their effectiveness for asthma. The goal will be to test these inhalers on the virtual lung instead of human beings. If all goes as planned, Dr. Kaul should be able to get very precise results very quickly. This is a good example if "in silico" or "organs-on-a-chip" research, which is poised to revolutionize clinical trials and drug discovery.

The other area where AI is making a big difference in the development of new drugs and innovative treatment protocols coming out of the biotech sector is that it provides medical researchers with a much better way of screening candidates for clinical trials, which can enormously streamline the entire research process.

Finding qualified candidates for clinical trials has always been a difficult process. At any given time, there are maybe three hundred thousand or more clinical trials going on in the U.S. The main source of participants for the trials is clinicians who see a particular patient and, given their condition, the practitioner matches the patient with a trial that they could be a good candidate for. This matching process works for the patients who need care and for the researchers who need the right kind of subjects for their clinical trials. But as you can imagine, there is an element of "hit or miss" in that process. Then, even once a person is identified as a possible candidate for a given clinical trial, there is a complicated exclusion and inclusion process that the hospital must put the patient through before they can make the final determination if they indeed qualify for the trial.

AI can take all of those elements out and much more precisely match subjects and researchers. The algorithm very quickly can run the exclusion and inclusion criteria, and then the patient can be matched to the clinical trial. The way most clinical trials work is that a pharmaceutical company or a biotech company partners with a given hospital or university system to find participants among their patients. AI can comb through millions of patient records and isolate those few patients in their database that qualify for the very stringent requirements of any particular study. This has not really been implemented yet, but there are companies working on it.

Benefits of AI to Insurance Companies

Think of the insurance industry, and particularly health insurance, and "efficiency" is not usually the first word that comes to mind. Instead, most of us think of health insurance providers as big, bloated bureaucracies that have trouble doing anything! AI is changing all that.

AI is already being used quite extensively in the insurance industry for data-driven tasks such as claims processing, underwriting, and fraud detection. Traditional insurance companies have started to embrace the technology, and we are seeing a lot of AI start-ups specializing in AI applications for the insurance industry, and in particular, for the processing of health insurance and benefits.

Some of those we have partnered with have to do with streamlining the "pre-approval process." This is something that hospitals have to deal with every day. If you check into a hospital, the hospital has to get "pre-authorization" for your length of stay from your insurance company before they admit you. That pre-authorization is based on history and actuarial models based on average rates of stays for your given condition or set of symptoms. As you have probably learned by now, running that kind of predictive model is what AI excels at. If this pre-authorization for the length of stay is not done accurately, it negatively impacts both the patient's health as well as the hospital's resources. AI is making this process much more accurate, maximizing both patient outcomes and the hospital's ability to allocate bed space and other critical assets.

Benefits of AI to Patients

Perhaps the most important stakeholder in healthcare is the patient. How AI is helping the other three stakeholders ultimately improves patient care and patient outcomes. But there are incredible innovations already in play where AI is having a more direct impact on patients in terms of diagnosis, prognosis, and treatment.

We can see a prime example of how this is currently working and a glimpse at what the future will bring by looking at what has gone on during the COVID-19 crisis. Since the lockdowns and massive quarantines that started around April of 2020, we saw the number of people leveraging telemedicine appointments skyrocket. This was driven by necessity, of course, but it has opened the door to a fundamental change in the way people perceive healthcare. They now have seen that for many situations, there is no need to see a doctor; telemedicine visits work. Also, people have gotten comfortable with using diagnostic apps that allow you to, for example, take a picture of a mole on your skin with your smartphone, and the app will tell you whether or not it is something to worry about. These kinds of things are largely AI-driven, and they are paving the way to a future of interacting with AI more often, and humans less often, when receiving healthcare. Also, this is being facilitated by the fact that out of necessity, insurance companies began reimbursement for telemedicine consultants. We are seeing the very foundations of AI inpatient care being built right now.

We are at an extremely critical junction right now, where all the variables are coming together—AI, smartphones, telemedicine, and the insurance companies getting onboard with it. While it may have come out of a bad situation (and innovation often does), the COVID-19 crisis has really helped get over one of the main hurdles that patients have with AI—the trust factor. People have this science fiction fear of machines. There is a fundamental mistrust of wanting to "speak to a human" when it comes to medical decisions. But, when hundreds of thousands of people were forced to do exactly that during the pandemic, they came to realize that this isn't so bad. The tying in of telemedicine and AI apps with smartphone platforms had a lot to do with that. For many, especially those of the millennial generation who are now getting older and needing more access to healthcare, the smartphone is a "trusted friend." They do everything on their phones, so why not access healthcare?

The necessary increase yet successful use of telemedicine apps during the pandemic has proven to people that this is something we can use and that we can trust. These hands-on experiences have shown them the truth behind AI in healthcare. AI is not there to replace or supplant doctors and nurses, but it is actually a powerful tool that helps clinicians do their jobs better. With AI, it is not that you will never see a doctor again, but you will only see a doctor when you really have to. And when you do, by the time you have gotten to see him or her, you will have been "triaged," so to speak, by AI, and the doctor will already know what your problem is and how to better treat it. It saves time and money and delivers better patient care.

There has been this distrust of AI in healthcare, but if you understand that this is something that is designed to augment your doctor's abilities—almost give him superpowers if you will—then you realize that AI is not something to distrust but rather, to embrace. Look at it this way. If you hire an architectural firm to build your house, you are not going to be worried or upset if you know he has used the latest in CAD/CAM and engineering software to design your house. You are going to say, "Great. I know this will be safe and sturdy, and the roof is not going to collapse." You need to think of AI in healthcare the same way, as simply the latest tool in a long line of technological advancements that are helping clinicians to deliver better patient care.

This is already becoming most apparent with medical devices and how they are evolving into smart machines through AI. Smart medical devices are already making an incredible difference in the delivery of patient care. I was able to see this firsthand in my father's case.

When he was in intensive care for twenty-one days, he was on a ventilator. Since COVID-19, ventilators have been in the news, and people have become far more aware of them and just what a lifesaving machine they can be. A ventilator is an extraordinarily complex piece of machinery. It is basically keeping you alive and breathing for you when your lungs cannot provide enough oxygen to your brain and other critical organs. It requires very subtle and precise monitoring of the patient on the ventilator, constant adjustments by the staff to make sure they are getting just the right amount of oxygen and are only on the machine for the safest length of time. There is only a certain number of days that a patient can be on a ventilator before it can start to have long-term negative effects on their body and brain. Adding an AI element to a medical device like a ventilator takes out much of the guesswork from the picture. With AI embedded, the machine learns how the patient breathes and constantly adjusts itself to their needs.

You can imagine what a difference that AI made during a crisis like the pandemic when there was, and continues to be, a shortage of ventilators. AI can make sure that only the patients that really need to be on ventilators are—and only for the time necessary, thus maximizing the use of a critical resource during a public health crisis.

As you can see, right now, the marriage of AI and medical device technology is where there is a world of opportunity for innovation, particularly in the area of imaging and diagnostics; it is becoming much more mainstream.

Karley Yoder, general manager and chief digital officer of ultrasound at GE Healthcare, recently said, "Within healthcare, solutions like AI and machine learning are revolutionizing the way healthcare data is analyzed and delivered. With these tools properly leveraged, we can enhance efficiencies, value, and outcomes, while reducing risk and clinical variation, all the while putting the patient first. To succeed, AI must be built and deployed the right way, ethically, with the right volume, variety, and veracity of data, and be embedded invisibly within the clinician's workflow. This is our focus at GE Healthcare, and we're already seeing it become a reality."

She is right. For example, currently there is a company, Digital Diagnostics, that is quite active in leveraging AI technology to detect and diagnose illness.

Digital Diagnostics first made headlines for getting Food and Drug Administration approval for a medical device that uses AI to detect diabetic retinopathy—without input from a doctor. It was the first such device to receive FDA approval. Now, the company is working on an AI system to detect skin cancer.

When they received their first FDA approval, the company was known as IDX for "eye diagnostics." Now they are looking at the big picture and how they can expand their solutions beyond eye care. That is the vision behind the company's recent rebranding as Digital Diagnostics, as it plans to continue to expand into medical specialties beyond its initial focus on eyes. As part of the rebranding, the company purchased 3Derm Systems and is now looking to adapt 3Derms technology to the early detection of breast cancer.

Another company, Overjet, recently announced that it raised nearly $8 million in funding to advance its AI solution for dentistry. Their technology merges dental imaging devices with AI and allows dentists to be far more accurate in detecting even subtle problems with a patient's teeth and develop better treatment plans based on a more detailed analysis of dental images that only AI can give.

These are just a few examples where AI is making a direct impact at the point of patient care. But there is another way that AI is enhancing the patient experience more globally. AI can address what have been major concerns about disparities in healthcare.

For decades, from advanced treatments such as vaccines or innovative technologies such as robotic surgery, America has often been at the cutting edge of advancements in healthcare. It is also an unfortunate truth of American medicine that these advancements are slow to trickle down where they are needed most, in communities of color. Globally, of course, this is also true, where such technology rarely finds its way into undeveloped nations. AI is changing all of that. Part of the magic of AI is that it does not require the doctor or the medical diagnostic device to be directly at the point of patient care. Look again to the tremendous uptick in telemedicine appointments during the pandemic. AI brings medicine to where the patients are, not the other way around.

With AI, you have a technology—regulations hurdles notwithstanding—that effectively can eliminate demographic and geographic borders to medicine, making top-notch healthcare and diagnostics far more accessible. Imagine what a difference this can make in places like India, where I have family and have seen this firsthand, where a given doctor could have forty or more patients in his waiting room at any one time.

We are also working in collaboration with Eric Sigel of Citadel Discovery. Citadel is using AI to accelerate drug discovery manyfold. Citadel Discovery is a public benefit corporation with the goal to generate and provide access to the data needed for applying AI to small molecule therapeutic discovery. Eric's primary focus is on DNA-Encoded Libraries (DELs), a technology that permits the generation of hundreds of millions of data points across libraries of molecules that can reach tens of billions of chemical entities. Over the past decade, Eric and his team have developed analysis tools for using this data to identify molecules for use in drug discovery programs.

The results of this work have spurred renewed and expanded interest into DELs and their application to identifying and optimizing active molecular series. Citadel's efforts are focused on democratizing access to this information rich data across the full range of thousands of human disease-relevant proteins with the goal to democratize access and enable industry and academia to advance understanding of the chemical biology needed to treat and cure diseases.

Where Can This Take Us?

At first glance, it is easy to see the clinical implications of AI and how it can improve patient care in terms of diagnostics and treatment. But as you can see, AI runs the gamut and can approve the delivery of healthcare across all of the major stakeholders in the industry.

It all comes down to this: The delivery of healthcare from the researcher to the clinician to the administrator is all about obtaining massive amounts of the best data available, then using their respective intellects, skills, and experiences to interpret that data to predict the best outcome for the patient. At its most fundamental level, AI is an immensely powerful prediction tool. That is what AI does best. It looks at huge data sets and has the ability to interpret that data with a high degree of success in predicting outcomes on orders of magnitude far greater than any human.

> **It all comes down to this: The delivery of healthcare from the researcher to the clinician to the administrator is all about obtaining massive amounts of the best data available, then using their respective intellects, skills, and experiences to interpret that data to predict the best outcome for the patient.**

Healthcare is a prime example of an industry where AI is not only improving or enhancing current systems and methods, it is also paving the way for unique and innovative protocols and technologies. AI is helping the industry to both survive and thrive. It is for that reason that there is such a dramatic opportunity for investment and start-ups in AI for healthcare.

TAKEAWAYS

- AI is exceptionally good at analyzing large sets of data and making very intuitive and accurate predictions based on the same.

- AI is already in place in many touchpoints in healthcare and is benefiting every major stakeholder in the industry: providers, pharma/biotech, insurers, and patients.

- As AI evolves, it is creating great opportunities for start-ups involving AI and healthcare, particularly in the areas of drug discovery, disease detection, and diagnostics.

Now that we understand a little bit more about where AI in healthcare is currently, let's begin to take a look at where it is going and how it is evolving, with a deep dive into developments in Natural Language Processing.

CHAPTER 2

Natural Language Processing–Beyond Speech to Text

Nobody phrases it this way, but I think that artificial intelligence is almost a humanities discipline. It's really an attempt to understand human intelligence and human cognition.

—SEBASTIAN THRUN

One of the cornerstones of AI and how it is currently being used and how it will further evolve in the future, particularly in healthcare, is Natural Language Processing, or NLP.

NLP allows machines to break down and interpret human language. It's at the core of many of the digital tools we use every day—from translation software, chatbots, spam filters, and search engines to grammar correction software, voice assistants, and social media monitoring tools.

Every time that you ask Siri or Alexa for anything, you are engaging with NLP. The better that those AI algorithms can understand the nuances of human language, the better they can respond to your questions.

> **At its core, Natural Language Processing is how machines learn to automatically understand and analyze huge amounts of unstructured text data, like social media comments, customer support tickets, online reviews, news reports, and more.**

At its core, Natural Language Processing is how machines learn to automatically understand and analyze huge amounts of unstructured text data, like social media comments, customer support tickets, online reviews, news reports, and more.

In the healthcare space, that is critical because so much of the data that doctors, administrators, researchers, and insurance companies, etc. deal with, is exactly that—unstructured and from many diverse sources. You have doctors' notes, phone texts, emails, handwritten text, voicemail messages—a whole host of information that resides in unstructured or natural language that needs to be understood and processed very quickly for any AI application in healthcare—from drug discovery to diagnostics to patient care.

An NLP algorithm makes it possible to sort through large volumes of unstructured sources, producing both insights as well as correlating and connecting data.

Within the healthcare sphere, NLP can be applied in a variety of situations, from reducing preventable deaths as a result of medical errors to identifying clinical pathologies in medical research and drug discovery.

AI, NLP, and Patient Care

A great deal of information exists for any single patient. They are variously stored in electronic medical records, appointment and medical history, payment accounting, messages to and from physicians, and insurance claims data. Given the enormous volume of data, it is important to focus on information that creates value.

The general guideline for creating such value includes (1) resources, activities context, interactions, customer role; (2) cognitive responses; and (3) discrete emotions. The clinical touch points would be

- diagnosis

- treatment

- follow-up

- the application of preventive measures

Additionally, experiential data collected through surveys and observations are also important for long-term payoff, including

- patient satisfaction

- perceptions

- engagement

- preferences

The most important technology in extracting such a care pathway is Natural Language Processing, as much of the original data is in unstructured form.

For example, say someone calls a help desk or information call center, and they need to know how to obtain certain medication, or they need to describe problems they're having with their medication. Someone on the other side will be taking notes—only these notes are not on paper; they're going into the electronic system. Now multiply that call by hundreds of agents, over hundreds of days, speaking with thousands of patients, and suddenly there are a million notes that have been taken. What do you do with those? Who manages them? Who reads them? How do you extract meaning from them?

NLP tools allow machines to learn to sort and route information with little to no human interaction— quickly, efficiently, accurately, and around the clock.

That is where AI and NLP can and are making a huge difference. NLP tools allow machines to learn to sort and route information with little to no human interaction—quickly, efficiently, accurately, and around the clock.

NLP tools assist healthcare professionals with the review and analysis of medical documents in a repeatable, scalable way. NLP will help reduce workforce burnout and increase healthcare productivity, both in the back office and in clinical practice.

Using NLP algorithms, healthcare providers can now better coordinate valuable medical insights that are captured in unstructured text, such as vaccinations or medications, that may be overlooked as patients move through their healthcare journeys. NLP-based AI solutions can improve patient outcomes by lowering the likelihood of redundant bloodwork or other tests, reducing operational spending, and improving the entire patient-doctor experience.

One such system already in use is the Healthcare Natural Language API (application programming interface) that is part of Google's Cloud Healthcare API. In April of 2020, at the peak of the COVID-19 pandemic, Google made its Cloud Healthcare API available to the healthcare industry at large.

According to Google, "the Healthcare Natural Language API identifies medical insights in documents, automatically extracting knowledge about medical procedures, medications, body vitals, or medical conditions. By using machine learning, the API identifies clinically relevant attributes based on the surrounding context. For example, it discerns medications prescribed in the past from medications prescribed for the future, and it picks up the likelihood of a specific symptom or diagnosis, as captured in language nuances. It can also distinguish medical insights that pertain to the patient from information that pertains to a patient's relative."[1]

To facilitate analysis of medical insights at that kind of scale, the Healthcare Natural Language API leverages AI and NLP to automatically normalize medical information against an industry-standard knowledge base such as Medical Subject Headings (MeSH) or International Classification of Diseases (ICD).

Again, NLP is essential for analysis at this level because of the richness and subtleties of human language—particularly in the medical field—that is often filled with overlapping meaning, yet analysis necessitates standardized data inputs. For example, the medical condition

---

1   Andreea Bodnari, "Healthcare Gets More Productive with New Industry-specific AI Tools," cloud.google.com, accessed January 2022, https://cloud.google.com/blog/topics/healthcare-life-sciences/now-in-preview-healthcare-natural-language-api-and-automl-entity-extraction-for-healthcare.

"diabetes" is commonly referred to as diabetes mellitus, while croup is also called *laryngotracheobronchitis* in specialist terms.

"With the Healthcare Natural Language API, similar medical information gets normalized into a standardized medical knowledge graph," says Google.

An Essential Power of Natural Language Processing

One of the most fascinating things about NLP algorithms and what makes them so powerful is that they can be tailored to your particular needs and criteria, like complex, industry-specific language, even sarcasm and misused words. This means that among our aforementioned healthcare stakeholders, NLP and AI can be drilled down to very specific language for specific applications.

For example, the Department of Defense is working in conjunction with the Health and Human Services Inspector General that leverages NLP to help identify health insurance fraud.

AI coupled with NLP can be very useful in recognizing fraud because of NLP's innate ability for "anomaly detection." The relevant AI algorithm can be trained to recognize language consistent with fraud, such as a sudden change in the tone and vocabulary in an earnings report, new stories that show abnormal language, or irregular origination could be another suspicious sign that would get flagged. Other clues can come from the "transparency" of earning calls, where frequent use of numbers, shorter words, and unsophisticated vocabulary is found to be correlated with high expectations in performance.

Healthcare fraud is considered extremely challenging for Medicaid, Medicare, and the general healthcare industry. The National Heath

Care Anti-Fraud Association estimates conservatively that healthcare fraud costs the nation about $68 billion annually—about 3 percent of the nation's $2.26 trillion in healthcare spending. Other estimates range as high as 10 percent of annual healthcare expenditure, or $230 billion.[2] This is a bloated expense to the nation, and hence, it becomes extremely crucial to address how to minimize this wasteful expenditure. More worrisome is that this abuse and fraud has made the total cost of healthcare increase substantially over the past few decades.

AI and NLP algorithms are redefining the way fraud detection is done these days. Before the advent of AI, the fraud prevention systems relied upon set patterns and analyzed only restricted fraud patterns.

NLP models coupled with AI algorithms can be used to instantly analyze thousands of past fraudulent claims in order to detect claims with similar language patterns and attributes and flag them before they are paid, saving millions of dollars.

And the savings are not only from not paying on fraudulent claims. NLP-based fraud detection helps AI to complete data analysis within milliseconds and detects complex patterns with a speed and efficiency that no human using typical fraud analytics could match.

AI removes time-consuming tasks and enables fraud analysts to focus on critical cases, like when risk scores are at their peak. The work quality and efficiency of fraud analysts also get enhanced since their workload uses automated AI algorithms.

Pharmaceutical companies are also using NLP's ability to very quickly and accurately mine insurance claims data to not only scour for fraud but also to improve patient care in several ways. Claims data is one area where the information on patients is complete and longitudinal. As such, it is a very valuable source for extracting insights

---

2   Blue Cross Blue Shield of Michigan, "Statistics," bcbsm.com, accessed January 2022, https://www.bcbsm.com/health-care-fraud/fraud-statistics.html.

that are important both for an individual patient and for the patient population at large.

By mining claims data, NLP can

- Spot trending diseases and conditions

- Identify the need for intervention for high-risk segments

- Identify gaps in medical treatment

- Identify poor health habits and promote health and wellness programs and patient education

This kind of insight extraction from claims data mining can lead to direct benefits to the pharmacy customer population.

Telemedicine and the Coronavirus Pandemic

The COVID-19 pandemic in many ways has raised awareness of the need and power of AI in medicine. It has also helped to illustrate some of its shortfalls and the challenges that remain. To ease the burden on strained emergency rooms and healthcare systems in general, not to mention to comply with quarantine protocols, thousands of Americans were forced into their first interaction with medical AI when using telemedicine.

Telehealth providers very quickly saw the value of Natural Language Processing. Telehealth companies found that they could deploy NLP algorithms to identify the most relevant symptoms, pre-existing conditions, and medications from a doctor-patient transcribed conversation.

Another lesson learned from the pandemic related to AI and NLP was the globalization of healthcare. To combat the pandemic, clinicians and researchers have had to share data from all over the world, and much of that also includes in-person as well as telemedicine doctor-patient interaction from across the globe. NLP is playing a critical role in healthcare in general, and in slowing the pandemic, specifically, in its ability to do robust real-time translations.

The possibility of translating text and speech to different languages has always been one of the main goals of NLP development. From the first attempts to translate text from Russian to English in the 1950s to state-of-the-art deep learning neural systems, machine translation—another aspect of machine learning and AI—has evolved considerably.

Google Translate, Microsoft Translator, and the Facebook Translation App are just a few examples of generic machine translation apps you have likely interfaced with. In August 2019, the Facebook AI English-to-German machine translation model received first place in the contest held by the Conference of Machine Learning. The translations obtained by this model were defined by the organizers as "superhuman" and considered highly superior to the ones performed by human experts.

But what makes machine translation so important to AI in healthcare has to do with customizable machine translation systems, which are adapted to a specific domain and trained to understand the terminology associated with a particular field, such as medicine.

AI, NLP, and Medical Research

Advances in Natural Language Processing are not only at the core of how AI is evolving in patient care; NLP serves a critical function in all sorts of medical research, and in particular, in drug discovery.

Pharmaceutical and biotechnology companies are recognizing the advantages of using NLP to streamline clinical trials by increasing the accuracy of patients matched against granular inclusion/exclusion protocol criteria.

Pharmaceutical researchers have long known that selection and recruiting techniques, paired with the inability to monitor and coach patients effectively during clinical trials, are two of the main causes for high trial failure rates.

NLP is a powerful drug discovery tool that has the ability to help researchers identify connections in their data more quickly and accurately. It can be used for assessing market potential, targeting patient populations correctly with existing drugs as well as finding new ones— all much faster than humanly possible.

Researchers often struggle to find the right participants for their clinical trials. Most studies have very specific requirements, and it is imperative that these studies not only enroll enough participants but that these volunteers meet the proper inclusion criteria as well.

Electronic Health Records (EHR) are the goldmine for the kinds of information that researchers need to match potential candidates with apropos clinical trials. But, because of the large volume of data documented in EHRs, the typical recruiting processes used to find relevant information can be extremely labor-intensive.

NLP-driven AI algorithms are now being used to search EHR data to rapidly screen potential candidates. By leveraging NLP and machine learning technologies, researchers are able to rapidly

analyze different types of data and automatically determine patients' suitability for clinical trials.

Beyond a better way of matching up the best candidates for a given clinical trial, NLP and AI are reshaping traditional drug discovery in many other ways. NLP is a powerful drug discovery tool that has the ability to help researchers identify connections in their data more quickly and accurately. It can be used for assessing market potential, targeting patient populations correctly with existing drugs as well as finding new ones—all much faster than humanly possible.

Thanks to its versatility, NLP now finds application at every level of research, including preclinical studies, design phase clinical trials, analysis post-approval monitoring programs, etc. NLP can analyze data and make connections faster than its human counterparts, saving both time and money.

We will dive much deeper into AI and drug discovery in Chapter 7.

Where Can This Take Us?

NLP will be the catalyst that takes AI in medicine to its ultimate promise. My colleagues and I are already developing an NLP-based AI algorithm for diagnostics and planned maintenance of helicopters and other high-value aircraft.

Basically, what our proposal does is take all of the technical manuals of that very sophisticated aircraft as well as anecdotal and other information from in-the-field repair technician and engineers notes, etc. that may be in natural language, and the NLP algorithm can ingest all of that data and create an NLP-driven repair manual that is overlaid with a Siri-like voice assistant. So, now any technician experiencing any issue with a system or part of the aircraft can simply ask the helicopter itself, "How do I fix this 'XYZ'?" in natural language and get a response on exactly how it is to be repaired, also in simple-to-understand, natural language.

Here is the really fascinating part: what we are proposing, and so far, has been very well received, not only leverages AI and NLP to understand everything about the maintenance and repair of the aircraft, it can monitor every mechanical part and every circuit and sensor and provide predictive maintenance. In other words, the AI built into the aircraft will know when the given part is nearing the end of its operational lifespan and warn the engineer or technician that this given part needs to be replaced before it becomes an issue.

We are also working with a start-up that is in the development of a similar program for the auto industry. Both of these concepts use NLP and AI to create what amounts to a virtual digital twin of the car or aircraft in question. It is not too much of a stretch from there to envision such a program that uses an NLP algorithm working in conjunction with a Fitbit, smartphone or other device that can detect biological changes within your body and "warn" you when something is wearing out and needing medical attention, or better yet digitally connect to your physician and automatically schedule a needed appointment or test for you!

NLP played a significant role in healthcare even before the large-scale adoption of AI we are seeing today. One of the earliest large-scale NLP applications in healthcare was the introduction of Nuance "speech to text" software known as Dragon. Dragon revolutionized the tedious process of having someone translate doctors' notes into text. With Dragon, the clinician merely could speak his notes as he would traditionally into a tape machine to later be translated, and they would be automatically digitized into text and saved on a computer.

Nuance, the company that created Dragon, was a pioneer in NLP, and since its introduction, has become a leading provider of NLP-based AI and cloud-based ambient clinical intelligence for healthcare providers. In April of 2021, Microsoft announced its acquisition of Nuance.

In a press release announcing the acquisition, Satya Nadella, CEO of Microsoft, said, "Nuance provides the AI layer at the healthcare point of delivery and is a pioneer in the real-world application of enterprise AI. AI is technology's most important priority, and healthcare is its most urgent application. Together, with our partner ecosystem, we will put advanced AI solutions into the hands of professionals everywhere to drive better decision-making and create more meaningful connections, as we accelerate growth of Microsoft Cloud for Healthcare and Nuance."

The fact that Microsoft recently acquired Nuance is just one more indication of how important the link between NLP, AI, cloud solutions, and the delivery of healthcare will be in the years ahead.

TAKEAWAYS

NLP is a driving force behind the current and future applications of AI in healthcare because:

- Natural Language Processing helps machines automatically understand and analyze huge amounts of unstructured text data.

- Natural Language Processing tools can help machines learn to sort and route information with little to no human interaction quickly, efficiently, accurately.

- Natural Language Processing algorithms can be tailored to any need or criteria, like complex, industry-specific language or targeting certain keywords, which has vast applications in AI for healthcare.

- Although NLP and AI in the healthcare field overall have reached remarkable milestones, there are many challenges that remain before the ultimate promise of AI and healthcare can become a reality. One of those is how to handle the enormity of the entire sphere of medical knowledge and research data that exists. Quantum computing may hold the answer.

CHAPTER 3

Quantum Computing–Speeding Up the Cycle

The promise of artificial intelligence and computer science generally vastly outweighs the impact it could have on some jobs in the same way that, while the invention of the airplane negatively affected the railroad industry, it opened a much wider door to human progress.

—PAUL ALLEN

You have all heard the term "quantum leap" and understand that it means an advancement that is miles, even lightyears, ahead in something. That certainly applies to the word's use in the emerging field of "quantum computing." Quantum computing is as far removed from conventional computing as a word processing program is from a lead pencil!

Quantum computers leverage the science and physics of quantum mechanics. This makes quantum computers orders of magnitude more powerful than even the most powerful supercomputers in use today. As a report by IBM—the developers of quantum computing—put it: "IBM designed quantum computers to solve complex problems that today's most powerful supercomputers cannot solve, and never will."[3]

Google has a quantum computer that they claim is 100 million times faster than any of today's systems.

Because quantum computing is based on the near-mystical phenomena of quantum theory, it can be somewhat hard to explain and understand. However, the main difference between quantum computers and conventional computers is that they do not store and process information in the bits and bytes that we are familiar with, but rather in something else entirely, known as quantum bits, or "qubits."

All conventional computing comes down to streams of electrical or optical pulses representing *1*s or *0*s. Everything from your tweets and e-mails to your iTunes songs and YouTube videos are essentially long strings of these binary digits.

Qubits, on the other hand, are typically made up of subatomic particles such as electrons or photons. Quantum mechanics and other esoteric sciences like string theory are based on the sometimes-quirky relationships these subatomic particles have with one another.

Without getting beyond the scope of this discussion, qubits store and process data in quantum form, which means that instead of having to process bits of *1*s and *0*s in a strict linear fashion, qubits

---

3   IBM Institute for Business Value, "Exploring Quantum Computing Use Cases for Healthcare," ibm.com, accessed January 2022, https://www.ibm.com/thought-leadership/institute-business-value/report/quantum-healthcare.

can exist as millions of *1*s and *0*s *at the same time*, which accounts for the incredible speed of quantum computers.

Qubits also have the quantum property of "entanglement," something that Einstein himself called "spooky action at a distance." While even today's most brilliant quantum physicists do not entirely understand the phenomenon, when two quantum particles become entangled, they wind up reflecting or mirroring one another, and therefore both existing in the same state. But thanks to the bizarre phenomenon of entanglement, they continue to exist in that state, even once they are separated over great distances. The effect is at the base of many practical and theoretical applications of quantum theory.

A simple way of understanding "entanglement" is it is an interdependence based on a long and intimate relationship between the two particles, like a child who goes away to college across the country but still is "dependent" on the support of their parents.

In quantum computing, entanglement is what accounts for the nearly incomprehensible processing power and memory of quantum computers. In a conventional computer, bits and processing power are in a one-to-one relationship—if you double the bits, you get double the processing power, but thanks to entanglement, adding extra qubits to a quantum machine produces an exponential increase in its calculation ability.

Quantum entanglement allows qubits, which behave randomly, to be perfectly correlated with each other. Using quantum algorithms that exploit quantum entanglement, specific complex problems can be solved more efficiently than on classical computers.

It all sounds quite complex, and it is, but the reality is just as you do not currently have to be a computer engineer to use your desktop computer, tablet, or iPhone, you do not have to completely understand quantum mechanics to use quantum computers.

Not that you will be using them anytime soon. Quantum computers will not wipe out conventional computers—not in the near term anyway. Using a conventional machine will still be the easiest and most economical solution for tackling most problems. But quantum computers promise to power exciting advances in various fields, from materials science to pharmaceuticals research. Companies are already experimenting with them to develop things like lighter and more powerful batteries for electric cars and to help create novel drugs.

Quantum computing is still very much an emerging technology, with large-scale and practical applications still a ways off. However, the technology is steadily graduating from the lab and heading for the marketplace. In 2019, Google announced that it had achieved "quantum supremacy," IBM has committed to doubling the power of its quantum computers every year, and numerous other companies and academic institutions are investing billions toward making quantum computing a commercial reality.

The magnitude of difference of the computing power between traditional machines and quantum machines is extraordinarily high, and that is why it can be applied in many areas of healthcare. But where they are and most likely will make the greatest difference is in drug discovery. In pharma research, you need to test chemical and biological reactions and make predictions and draw conclusions from vast combinations of interactions on a molecular level. Which is exactly what the enormous speed and processing power of quantum computing was made for.

Quantum Computing and AI

Quantum computing will take AI and machine learning to the next level. The marriage between the two is an area to pay very close attention to for start-ups as well as for where Big Tech will be going over the next five to ten years.

Consider this: we are at the limits of the data processing power of traditional computers, and the data just keeps growing. It has been estimated that we produce 2.5 exabytes (one exabyte equals one billion gigabytes) of data every day. That's equivalent to two hundred fifty thousand Libraries of Congress or the content of 5 million laptops!

In order to handle this ever-increasing volume of data, there's a race from the biggest leaders in the industry to be the first to launch a practical quantum computer. Only a quantum computer will be powerful enough to process all of this Big Data and be able to solve increasingly complex problems in order for AI to reach its full potential.

The fact of the matter is: data is exploding. AI is very good at making accurate predictions based on being able to process vast amounts of data. However, conventional computers put a limit on just how much of the data can be processed. So, it is the computers themselves right now that are the greatest limiting factor to how far AI can go. Quantum computing is poised to change all of that.

Quantum computing algorithms will allow us to enhance what's already possible with machine learning. Remember how in the last chapter we talked about NLP and how it interfaces with AI to be able to analyze all kinds of unsorted data?

Quantum computing is expected to be able to search very large, unsorted data sets to uncover patterns or anomalies extremely quickly. That means that a quantum computer, to use one of the examples in our last chapter, looking to match candidates for a drug trial, could theoretically access all the candidates in a database at the same time to identify commonalities based on the inclusion criteria—in seconds!

AI is being used to do this today, but it still requires a parallel computer looking at every record one after another, so it takes an incredible amount of time relative to how quickly a quantum computer could do the same task.

The promise is that quantum computers will allow for quick analysis and integration of our enormous data sets, which will improve and transform our machine learning and artificial intelligence capabilities.

At its core, AI and machine learning are science's attempts to make machines "think" like the human brain. As stated earlier, conventional computers "think," (i.e., process information) in a linear fashion—that series of *1*s and *0*s. But the human brain doesn't really think in a linear fashion; it thinks more in an algorithmic fashion, drawing complex connections from millions of neurons firing off all at the same time, more like the quantum cloud of daisy-chained particles in a quantum computer. And that is why quantum computing is so important to AI. It may be the path to the "holy grail" of computing—creating AI that processes information like a human brain, but even faster and more accurately!

In a hypothetical or an esoteric sense, there really isn't an upper limit to AI. Just like there really is no upper limit to human interpretation or understanding.

Currently, the only limit on AI is the limitation of the machine to actually learn. Quantum computing has the ability to eliminate that limitation or greatly expand on it such that, just like a human, there really is no limit to what you or the machine can learn.

However, I am not describing the typical science fiction scenario of AI replacing humans. Rather, I like to say that AI is giving human beings a true "superpower" because no matter how sophisticated or "smart" AI becomes, a human will always be in the loop.

Quantum Computing and Healthcare

It is easy to see how healthcare is one industry that holds a lot of potential to integrate quantum computing. In fact, it is an industry greatly in need of quantum computing. Perhaps more so than any other business, healthcare is extremely driven by Big Data—you've got clinical trials, disease registries, diagnostics, electronic health records, on and on and on. It's a very complex system, and it's not hard to see how it can easily challenge even the best capabilities of classical computing systems.

Quantum's ability to compute exponentially will allow clinicians to incorporate a vast number of cross-functional data sets into their patient risk factor models. The smallest minutia that might originally be overlooked—like the impact on their health of pollution levels in the air or water system where a patient lives—will be picked up because quantum can include environmental data and weather patterns in its analysis.

Another way quantum's computer power will vastly improve patient care is in its ability to process imagery at scale. Analyzing images, such as CT scans, requires much more processing power than traditional data sets. With increased power and speed made available by quantum computing, clinicians could more easily review CT scans of a patient that may have been taken over time, for example—monthly or yearly cancer screenings—and very quickly identify changes and anomalies. In this way, quantum computers will help health professionals to detect disease at earlier stages.

By using quantum-driven AI algorithms, oncologists will be able to make diagnoses with greater precision, increasing performance and reducing costs.

According to an IBM white paper[4] on quantum computing and healthcare, quantum computing will impact healthcare in three key areas:

1. Diagnostic assistance: Diagnose patients early, accurately, and efficiently

2. Precision medicine: Keep people healthy based on personalized interventions/treatments

3. Pricing: Optimize insurance premiums and pricing.

Diagnostic assistance has already been discussed in the example above. Precision medicine aims to tailor prevention and treatment approaches to the individual. Unfortunately, current medical care does not have the ability to be all that precise. Due to the complexity of human biology, individualized medicine requires considering aspects that go well beyond standard medical care. As a result, many existing therapies fail to achieve their intended effects due to individual variability. For example, according to the IBM report, only a third of patients respond to drug-based cancer therapies. In some cases, consequences of drug therapies can be disastrous; in Europe alone, up to two hundred thousand people die each year due to adverse drug reactions. However, imagine a scenario where

---

4   Dr. Frederik Flöther, "Exploring quantum computing use cases for healthcare," IBM, accessed December 2022, https://www.ibm.com/thought-leadership/institute-business-value/report/quantum-healthcare.

the power of a quantum-based AI could compare the pharmacopeia database along with the human genome and your individual DNA, and you have a vast potential to realize the vision of completely precise individualized medicine.

While it may not seem as sexy or exciting as improved diagnostics and advanced individualized medicine, the third area where quantum is ready to make a major difference in healthcare is pricing, and according to IBM, it may be just as critical.

One key area in which quantum computing may help optimize pricing is risk analysis, and it actually ties back to the precision medicine aspect. Since quantum computing can help to better assess the risk a given patient has for the development of a given medical condition. Leveraging these insights about predispositions and disease risk at the population level and then combining them with quantum risk models that can compute financial risk more efficiently could allow health plans to achieve improved risk and pricing models.

As we illustrated in the example given in our discussion of NLP, another area where quantum computing may support pricing decisions is enhanced fraud detection.

Why is the benefit of quantum to price modeling important? Enhanced fraud detection could save billions of dollars and waste in the healthcare system, and using quantum to better analyze pricing decisions could lower healthcare premiums for everyone.

When it comes to quantum computing and healthcare, quantum-enhanced machine learning algorithms stand out for the extensiveness of their applications. This is because we are at a time when the health and medical-related datasets are increasingly expansive, unsorted, and unevenly distributed—producing complex computational challenges even for the currently most-advanced supercomputers and AI.

Quantum Computing and Drug Discovery

In the not-too-distant future, quantum computing may provide life-saving medical applications we have never seen the likes of before. But, for now, its greatest implications are and will be in the arena of drug discovery.

Current drug discovery is extraordinarily time-consuming, with huge costs and a large number of processes, often taking many years of laboratory experiments and clinical trials. A new drug typically takes ten to fifteen years to progress from discovery to launch, and the capitalized costs exceed $2 billion. The success rate is less than 10 percent from entry into clinical development to launch. But, with quantum computing, it will be feasible to simulate the effect of different chemical compounds on organisms at the molecular level, which will reduce costs while making the whole process considerably easier.

> **But, with quantum computing, it will be feasible to simulate the effect of different chemical compounds on organisms at the molecular level, which will reduce costs while making the whole process considerably easier.**

The interest in quantum computing for drug discovery is not just about the hype. The impetus and the funding are in place, especially with COVID in the picture, for more forward-looking technologies that emphasize time to result—something that quantum computing has going for it.

Molecular dynamics (MD) and related methods are close to becoming routine computational tools for drug discovery. While MD codes have impressive scalability on the world's largest supercomputers, with quantum, there is—in theory—no limit to the number of molecules that can be run through in a single simulation via quantum methods. Not only will the results be delivered far faster—nearly instantaneously—the limits of computational capacity would no longer be a constraint to assessing targets.

Remember in our earlier discussion how we explained that, rather than working in isolation, qubits become entangled and act as a group, which helps enable quantum computers to achieve an exponentially higher information density and computing speed than classical computers? This gives them an advantage over classical computers in solving four types of problems: combinatorial optimization, differential equations, linear algebra, and factorization—making it ideal for MD. Whereas modeling penicillin on a classical computer would take 1,086 bits, it could take as few as 286 qubits on a quantum computer.

According to CB Insights, another area where drug discovery could see a boost from quantum computing is protein folding. Start-up ProteinQure—which was featured by CB Insights in the 2020 cohorts for the AI 100 and Digital Health 150[5]—is already tapping into current quantum computers to help predict how proteins will fold using conventional computers. But using quantum computing to address the issue could ultimately make designing powerful protein-based medicines easier.

Quantum computing can also enhance the screening processes used in early drug discovery. Virtual screening tools tend to be cheaper and faster than chemical processes for screening large compound libraries against a target of interest. But the usefulness

5   CB Insights, "Digital Health 150 of 2020: The Digital Health Startups Transforming the Future of Healthcare," cbinsights.com, accessed January 2022, https://www. cbinsights.com/research/digital-health-startups-redefining-healthcare-2020/.

of virtual tools depends on their ability to accurately predict hits, especially for complex molecules. Quantum computing has the potential to transform virtual screening through physically precise modeling of drug-target interactions and efficient screening of massive virtual libraries. Another complication is that building a tool to test compounds for the desired impact on a target during screening is a slow, labor-intensive lab process. By improving virtual or computer-modeled screening (in silico) compound testing, quantum computing could reduce the need for costly and time-consuming in vitro testing. Eventually, quantum computing could permit completely end-to-end in silico drug discovery.

Boehringer Ingelheim, a large European research and drug discovery company, recently became the first pharma company to partner with Google for quantum computing efforts. The drug discovery giant also created an internal lab to collaborate on how AI and quantum will integrate with their current pharma research and development plans.

"Quantum computing has the potential to significantly accelerate and enhance [research and development] processes in our industry. Quantum computing is still very much an emerging technology. However, we are convinced that this technology could help us to provide even more humans and animals with innovative and ground-breaking medicines in the future," Michael Schmelmer, member of the board of managing directors of Boehringer Ingelheim, said when the partnership was announced.

Interestingly enough, Google recently announced that it had used a quantum computer to simulate a chemical reaction, a milestone for the nascent technology.

Boehringer is far from the only biotech company pinning its hopes on quantum and AI. Roche has a general article about quantum on its website. Novartis CEO lists quantum along with other tech trends like telemedicine and believes it is just over the horizon. There has been buzz about interest in in-house quantum labs at Pfizer, Johnson & Johnson, and Merck, among others.

Time to market is everything in drug discovery; as we will learn more about in Chapter 7, AI speeds up just about every aspect and every phase of the drug discovery process, from molecular dynamics modeling to clinical trial recruitment. And as we have just learned in this chapter, quantum computing enhances every aspect of AI.

Biopharma companies have the potential to benefit significantly from this technology, and those that begin taking the right steps now may gain a lasting advantage. Anyone reading this book who is interested in developing a start-up based on an AI algorithm for healthcare should be seriously setting their sights on applications leveraging quantum computing in pharma and biotech. The same goes for investors!

TAKEAWAYS

- Quantum computers can analyze huge data sets, process information, and solve complex problems orders of magnitude faster than conventional computers. They can solve problems that ordinary computers simply never will be able to.

- Quantum computers are the bridge between AI and NLP that can take machine learning to an extraordinary level, improving healthcare in three key areas: diagnostics, precision medicine, and medical research.

- Quantum computing is likely to have its largest impact in the world of medicine in how it will accelerate drug discovery and the creation of more targeted therapeutics.

If we connect the dots between AI, NLP, and quantum computing, it will draw a direct line into our next chapter—one of the most fascinating aspects of AI—the creation and application of cognitive digital twins.

CHAPTER 4

Cognitive Digital Twin

General anatomical models based on population data do not capture the unique characteristics of your heart. A digital twin does.

—HENK VAN HOUTEN, EXECUTIVE VICE PRESIDENT, CHIEF TECHNOLOGY OFFICER, ROYAL PHILIPS

A cognitive digital twin (CDT) is a digital representation of a physical system that is augmented or enhanced by AI. It uses different AI technologies to continue learning and increase its capabilities over time. What makes a digital twin so valuable is that it has the ability to span the entire lifecycle—the health journey, if you will—of the component or system it is "twinning." When you combine that with AI, you have an incredibly powerful tool that is updated in real time while using machine learning and AI reasoning to gain more insights from the data, put it in the right context, and deliver incredibly accurate simulations that allow for confident decision making.

At the most basic level, a digital twin is a highly sophisticated virtual model that represents parts or the whole of the physical thing it represents. Sensors linked to the physical "thing" collect data in the real world that can be tracked by the virtual model. Anyone using the digital twin can now see crucial information—in real time—about how the physical thing is performing in the real world and use its simulation capabilities to predict how it might perform under specific circumstances in the future.

The digital twin concept isn't brand new. Dr. Michael Grieves introduced it in a paper he published in 2002, where he introduced the concept of creating a digital replica of a physical system in the context of product lifecycle management (PLM). He elaborated more in his book published in 2011, *Virtually Perfect: Driving Innovative and Lean Products through Product Lifecycle Management.* However, what is new is the connectivity, the huge datasets we have available, as well as the virtually unlimited computing power we have today that were only a vision when Greives first introduced the concept over two decades ago.

As you might imagine, long before anyone envisioned the idea of "twinning" a biological system, cognitive digital twins were used to test and maintain mechanical systems.

Today, digital twins are an integral part of designing, manufacturing, and operating some of the world's most high-value military and commercial systems, such as fleets of cars, ships, and aircraft.

In fact, our own first foray into the practical use of CDT was an application we developed for a global automotive client. My associates and I got involved with this client a few years ago. We were tasked with building a virtual representation model of the air spring in the car.

The air suspension system is the main load-carrying component on an automobile; therefore, it is integral to the safety and comfort of those in the vehicle. In high-performance cars such as those made by our client, it is also critical to that sportscar handling the driver expects. It is a complex part, consisting of an air compressor, an air-supply tank, leveling valves, check valves, bellows, piping, etc., and it is also a very high-value part. This all made it ideal for cognitive digital twinning.

Also, this part was in the automaker's new line of electric vehicles, which they were in the process of trying to gain market acceptability, so ensuring the public's perception of reliability and comfort was tantamount to their marketing efforts.

For some reason, in the EVs in particular, the air springs seemed to be failing in certain weather conditions, with different failure rates in different parts of the country, and the client's engineers were having a lot of troubles finding the root causes of the problem and under what conditions such problems might happen.

We put our data scientists on it, building a virtual CDT representation of all of the systems and subsystems of the air spring. Using AI capabilities and advanced machine learning algorithms, we were able to create the "health journey" of the spring, and we were able to predict with 90 percent certainty, the conditions under which it would fail.

Leveraging CDT technology, we were able to simulate and visually represent exactly how and where the springs were deteriorating. By monitoring the status of the air spring with digital twinning, now you can know the status of the system when the car comes in for routine maintenance or other repairs and take any necessary actions which by the way can be recommended by the CDT of this specific car. Or you can take preemptive action and call the vehicle in for repairs or corrections before a breakdown can happen out on the road.

According to the engineers with this specific client, dealership technicians were roughly 30 percent correct in diagnosing the actual failure on the air spring system. Meaning they were wrong 70 percent of the time! This led to significant increases in warranty repair costs and frustrated customers. Additionally, they had no way of knowing the health of the remaining components or of predicting when they might fail.

By contrast, our digital twin model was able to diagnose the system with a 96 percent accuracy, and our data science team estimated that number could be improved to above 98 percent. Our predictive capability is currently estimated at approximately 80 percent, and our data science team expects that number to improve to above 85 to 90 percent once the model is fully tuned.

The success we had with the air springs led us to develop a CDT algorithm for what you rightly would imagine is the highest value part in an electric vehicle—the battery.

We created a similar CDT model for the battery, and it has been working out very well.

Roll Out of CarTwin

The successful proofs of concept that we created for this automotive client for single subsystems like batteries and air springs and then extended to multiple systems with sensors for brakes, shocks, etc. led us to realize: Why not create a cognitive digital twin of the entire vehicle? We have done exactly that with a new venture we have recently launched, called—not surprisingly—CarTwin.

Basically, CarTwin can provide diagnostic and predictive models for all vehicle systems for which data is available (either directly or indirectly) onboard the vehicle. As an example, for the project with our OEM, we have already built models for the suspension, braking, and battery systems and are continuing to add additional systems as we move along. Our POC project will add the ignition system, fuel system, and turbocharging system. Virtually any part of the vehicle that has sensors or that sensors can be developed for can be "twinned." These data sets will be augmented with design and manufacturing data that is already available by the OEM.

CarTwin obtains its data from the "CAN Bus," which is basically the "communication network" on a vehicle that enables data acquisition, also in real time. CarTwin utilizes the data from the CAN Bus, as well as historical data about the inspection, repair, and parts replacement from the service centers to build our models. This means that it can be used in any vehicle that is newer than 1996, when the CAN Bus started to be used. It's worth noting as well that the more data that is available from any given vehicle as well as more vehicles, the better CarTwin can perform for at least all similar vehicles.

Depending on the sensor data available, CarTwin is not restricted to passenger cars. It can be used on trucks, special mobile equipment such as excavating equipment, motorcycles, boats, RVs, basically, anything that has a CAN Bus or similar diagnostics and computer monitoring interface.

Digital Twin Applications in Healthcare

Once you understand what a digital twin is and how they are being used to monitor and simulate functionality and wear and tear on mechanical systems, it is not too much of a leap to understand the enormous potential CDTs have in healthcare.

"Personalized medicine does not require only data; it requires more insights gained only through large amount of complex knowledge. Human Cognitive Twins will collect the required data about the patient, use relevant knowledge to put it in the right context, and if needed collaborate with other human and machines' twins to offer the best personalized healthcare services," so says my friend and colleague, Dr. Ahmed El Adl, founder of the Cognitive Digital Twin, PhD computer science (AI and robotics).

Of course, they are being used to twin high-value medical equipment just as they are being used for other mechanical devices, but there is a wealth of other potential when you think about the possibilities of creating digital representation for biological systems with cognitive digital twins.

The value of digital twins in the mechanical world is their ability, as we have done with our CarTwin, to provide incredibly real-time asset health monitoring and accurate predictive maintenance services involved in early failure predictions of high-value parts and complicated systems. Could we apply the same concept in healthcare? The answer is absolutely *yes*. It is not too hard to imagine how CDT technology could be used as a diagnostic and predictive tool providing the ultimate in personalized and preventive medicine.

Cardiovascular diseases (CVDs) take the lives of more than 18 million people every year—almost one-third of all deaths worldwide. CDT can enable a cardiologist to know when plaque is forming, clogging arteries at its earliest stages, and how it is affecting the health of the patient. Taking preventive actions at the right time would prevent expensive and risky bypass surgery. Another area for CDT in healthcare is diseases research, in general or for a specific patient. Detecting diseases like cancer in their earliest stage when interventions have the highest degree of success is a major area where CDT technology is adding lifesaving values.

This is not just theoretical. Digital twinning is already being used in different aspects of healthcare, maybe not to a great extent yet to model actual biological systems, but it is being used to design and create virtual representation and models to monitor the health and performance of implantable medical devices such as pacemakers.

Once you understand how a medical device such as a pacemaker is functioning and how it can be modeled to monitor its operational lifespan, you can then easily see how that can also be applied to any biomechanical device or surgical implant. It is not inconceivable how, in the near future, artificial knee or hip replacements, for example, will include sensors to their cognitive digital twins, which will monitor them for wear and tear and let surgeons know when they may need to be modified or replaced before a patient starts to feel pain or signs of immobility.

Taking the digital twin concept one step further in the realm of innovative implantable biomedical devices, digital twins can also be very useful in optimization tasks, such as upgrading or improving the device's performance by running hundreds of simulations with different conditions and different patients. Then, if we think about adding in 3D printing technology, we have a way that a patient's digital twin can lead to the personalization of such medical devices by creating unique 3D-printed designs for each patient's individual physiology!

But where the cognitive digital twin shows the most promise in healthcare is to emulate what we have done for individual car parts to virtually model individual human organs and use data to enable case simulation and prediction.

This revolution has already begun. There are multiple projects to create a Digital Twin for the human brain, either for the purpose of better understanding it or for the purpose of cognitive disease research and treatment. Hewlett Packard Enterprise, for example, partnered with Ecole Polytechnique Fédérale de Lausanne's (EPFL) on its Blue Brain Project, deploying its supercomputer to create digital models of the human brain for research purposes. In addition to that, both Siemens and Philips are working on versions of a virtual heart, using AI and CDT technology that allows cardiologists to evaluate several cardiac functions that are relevant to diagnosis and treatment of patients with cardiovascular disease. The CDT was pretrained on thousands of 2D ultrasound images of thousands of human hearts with or without CVD. Then, it uses the 2D heart ultrasound images of the patient to create an accurate model for their heart. That is another crucial lifesaving application of CDT in healthcare.

> **These kinds of "virtual organs" are and will revolutionize not only diagnostics and preventive medicine, but they will also have an astounding impact on research—allowing scientists to test drugs and conduct other clinical trials on "virtual bodies" that could perfectly mimic human physiology.**

These kinds of "virtual organs" are and will revolutionize not only diagnostics and preventive medicine, but they will also have an astounding impact on research—allowing scientists to test drugs and conduct other clinical trials on "virtual bodies" that could perfectly mimic human physiology.

Imagine the time and cost savings that could present over traditional drug discovery!

A Breakthrough for the Treatment of Lung Disease

If you recall from the introduction of this book, one of the driving forces that put me on the path to developing AI applications for healthcare was seeing my father succumb to lung disease. It is no coincidence then that one of the researchers we have collaborated with is Himanshu Kaul, PhD. Himanshu was recently awarded a nearly $700,000 grant to develop a "virtual lung" for use in clinical drug trials.

A virtual human lung is destined to be a game-changer in the development of new therapies and in the ways of caring for patients with all sorts of lung diseases. But for now, Dr. Kaul's virtual lung is being designed to virtually test the inhalers that are used for the treatment of patients with asthma.

In a March 2021 University of Leicester press release[6] announcing Dr. Kaul's research grant, he said, "lung diseases are a major source of socio-economic burden globally. My long-term research vision is to create software that will allow clinicians and pharmaceutical companies to predict how well a drug will perform in patients and offer a way to optimize its therapeutic efficacy."

One of the issues with developing effective therapeutics for patients with lung disease is that each individual's lungs seem to react somewhat differently to the drugs in the inhalers typically used to administer the aerosolized medication. By using his "virtual lung" Dr. Kaul believes he will be able to test real inhalers with real-world results without the need to test them on dozens of different asthma patients.

---

6   University of Leicester, "Virtual clinical trials could revolutionize the way new drugs are developed," le.ac.uk, March 5, 2021, https://le.ac.uk/news/2021/march/in-silico-lung.

According to the University press release,[7] using agent-based modeling, Dr. Kaul is collaborating with experts from the University of Leicester's Schools of Engineering and Mathematics and Department of Respiratory Sciences on his pioneering research project, titled *The Lung Pharmacome.*

The project aims to produce a working in silico lung by 2024, with the ambition of conducting patient-specific "virtual clinical trials" by 2025 at the earliest. The initial area of focus for the research will be lung diseases, specifically asthma and chronic obstructive pulmonary disease (COPD).

According to the Centers for Disease Control and Prevention, COPD affects more than 15 million Americans, and over 150,000 Americans die of COPD each year—that is, one death every four minutes. We see statistics like these because coming up with safe and effective therapies for lung diseases such as COPD can prove to be quite challenging. While a few such medications have been released in the last decade or so, the development of new medicines to treat lung disease is a highly expensive and risky process, and the failure rate is high.

Dr. Kaul and his team believe that, once fully developed, their virtual lung technology will be able to make highly accurate and timely predictions on target-specific and patient-specific therapeutic compounds. Further, the technology promises not only to hasten the time to get effective therapeutics into the hands of doctors, but it can also help to monitor the success of those drugs for specific patients over the course of their disease. Being able to drill down on a drug's effectiveness to such a personal level—will allow practitioners to customize treatment plans according to their patient's

---

7   Ibid.

unique needs and disease progression, ultimately improving their clinical outcomes.

Dr. Kaul's research is proving that a virtual human organ can provide more accurate, patient-specific predictions of the effectiveness of prescription drugs. He is also showing how "organs on a chip" can be used to analyze vast streams of individual lifestyle data, which will allow practitioners to gain a better understanding of the health implications of the choices patients make and, therefore, better project current and future outcomes.

Cognitive Digital Twins and Drug Discovery

The initial research done by Dr. Kaul and other research teams has proven the incredible value of in silica research to drug discovery. Using CDT models in place of actual patients can profoundly speed up the drug discovery process, saving time and money, while at the same time, eventually even totally eliminating the need to put any human being at risk of side effects or death during a clinical trial. The implications to the pharmaceutical industry are enormous, therefore, we see exponentially increasing investments to accelerate innovation and further develop the required products and services.

Combined with "Patient Digital Twin," CDT is going to make personalized healthcare possible and economically available to billions or people.

Combined with "Patient Digital Twin," CDT is going to make personalized healthcare possible and economically available to billions or people.

Traditional clinical trials take billions of dollars and years, if not decades, of hard work with no guarantee for the new drug to then be approved by regulatory bodies, not to mention the difficulties in finding the right participants for a trial and the risks to them once they do sign up.

When you read any medical research paper or article, you will come across the terms "in vitro" and "in vivo" to describe the studies. *In vitro* is Latin for "in glass." *In vivo* is Latin for "within the living." In research, the terms are used to describe whether the research was done "in the lab" in test tubes on tissue samples and such or in actual living animals or humans. CDT technology, as we have been describing, is ushering in a new type of experimentation with a new name—"in silico," which describes data using "organs on chips" or the "virtual organs" created using cognitive digital twins.

One of the promises of CDT is to make complete in silico drug trials a reality. Early successes occurring now are paving the way to a time in the not-so-distant future when no humans, nor animals, not even a single living cell will be required for drug discovery—and yet the impact of any given therapeutic or treatment option on a targeted organ or system can be perfectly charted.

The SIMULIA Living Heart project, which Dassault Systems and the U.S. Food and Drug Administration created in 2014, was one of the first studies to use CDT technology specifically to see the interaction of an organ with medicines. Originally designed as a five-year project, the collaboration with the U.S. Food and Drug Administration was recently extended for an additional five years.

This was one of the first studies specifically designed to run in silico trials to reduce the need to test new medicines on animals or humans. The SIMULIA Living Heart is a digital twin model of a human heart whose accuracy has been verified by various scientists, doctors, and engineers who are working on the project. One of the most fascinating aspects of the SIMULIA virtual heart is that it could be personalized to mimic the condition of specific patients.

Like any other aspect of AI-powered systems, digital twins of specific organs or biological systems are designed to continuously learn. A cognitive digital twin of an organ such as a human heart or lung that is being used for drug discovery by its very nature will become more accurate and patient-specific over time and therefore can be adjusted to almost any scenario that the researcher is looking into. Being AI-driven, the twinned virtual organ could conceivably come up with scenarios that the researchers themselves would never have thought of.

Right now, the use of digital twins in drug discovery is in its infancy, but its appeal to pharma is broad, and its use is expanding. Digital twins in pharma research can be found in use looking into anticoagulant and heart failure medications, novel drug delivery mechanisms for biologics, and precision electrical neurostimulation therapies.

Ubiquitous in silico drug trials may still be years away, but given our understanding of the concept and the capabilities we already have, it is just a matter of time before CDT-powered in silico drug research is going to be the norm.

Besides these few examples where digital twins are being used in drug discovery, where they are much more prevalent even now is in the designing and testing of medical devices. As you might imagine, it is far easier to twin an artificial heart valve—much as we did for the air spring on a car—than it is for a living organ with all of its biological and chemical complexities.

The Dassault virtual heart is being used to test many such devices, such as the designs of new, minimally invasive heart valves that must collapse to be safely installed, expand for a secure fit in a living, breathing environment, and must perform flawlessly to keep the patient alive.

Beyond modeling individual organs or biomechanical systems to emulate targets for a drug's effectiveness in treating a particular disease or defect, there is an equally remarkable aspect of digital twinning that could create massive change for the future of drug discovery and medical research.

Eventually, we will be able to use AI and CDT technologies to create a "virtual twin" of the doctor or scientist that is conducting the actual experiments. Imagine this: you have a virtual twin of the doctor that has all of his academic knowledge as well as every paper he has read, along with his practical experiences. Then that virtual twin is linked with the cognitive digital twin model that is being experimented on, and you have a "researcher" who can conduct experiments and make predictions with the speed and efficiency of AI, but that also has the "intuition" of its human brain and experiences to catch something in the nuance of the data being presented by the virtual organ!

With each model that is created and being put into use, digital twins are increasingly getting better at representing not only the functionality of the organ they have been designed to emulate but also the mechanism of action of the given therapy they are being used to investigate. Even now, digital twins of patients are growing in sophistication. As more biomarker and molecular data becomes available, it really is only a matter of time till we understand how to use all of that data to develop digital twins of real people.

The Virtual Patient

What is already being accomplished with the virtual heart and virtual in silico versions of various other parts of the body and its systems opens the door to the ultimate promise of CDT in healthcare: a computer model of *the entire human body*. A "virtual patient" that can use a digital twin to monitor your own health the same way that CDTs are currently used by the Department of Defense to provide predictive maintenance for helicopters and fighter jets!

One of the major steps toward an accelerated monetization of CDT in healthcare is to replace the current electronic medical record with a "CDT-based virtual patient." This patient CDT will receive all medical data including scans, tests, diagnostics, medication, and many other relevant data. It'll combine all of these data sets with domain knowledge and make it available to medical care teams as well as to other specialized CDTs.

Right now, all therapies—be they drugs, surgeries, or any other treatment modality—are designed to work as best as they can for the majority of patients. But that leaves large percentages of the population that do not respond to a given drug, and for them, there is often no relief for their suffering. According to the U.S. Food and Drug Administration (FDA),[8] the percentage of patients for whom medications are ineffective ranges from 38 to 75 percent for varying conditions from depression to osteoporosis.

The reason for this is simple. There are many things all humans share in common biologically, which makes this broad approach to medicine even possible. However, we are each genetic individuals, and

---

8   U.S. Food and Drug Administration, "Paving the Way for Personalized Medicine," published 2013, https://www.fdanews.com/ext/resources/files/10/10-28-13-Personalized-Medicine.pdf

that DNA specificity determines why a drug could work one way in one person and a different way or not at all in another. What if we could eliminate that guesswork? Having a cognitive digital twin of patients based on their unique genetic code and health history would eliminate any of that "hit or miss," and a doctor could theoretically test a given therapeutic—or indeed multiple therapeutics—on "your body" before prescribing the one that he or she knew would definitely work best for you. It is a fascinating and within-reach concept.

This kind of individualized digital twinning has implications well beyond drug actions or interactions. It can also be used before physical interventions such as laser therapies, radiotherapy, or surgical operations are performed on the patient, by using the twin to run various testing scenarios to make sure that the given procedure will be successful or is even necessary. It is a natural extension to surgical techniques widely used today, mainly in brain surgery such as MRI-guided brain surgery. The twin may be able to run some simulations and suggest less-invasive or noninvasive alternatives based on its knowledge of the person's individual physiology, supported by accumulated knowledge from similar past surgeries.

Basically, once fully realized, using CDT technology to create an individualized virtual twin of each of us will allow the application of the optimal treatment based on your unique needs. And, much as it is being used now in the mechanical world, CDT software can monitor your virtual doppelganger and alert you or your medical professionals before a medical condition arises—providing the ultimate in not only personalized medicine but in preventive medicine.

This is already being realized by marrying digital twins with connected wearable devices, and we will discuss this in far greater depth in our next chapter.

Where Can This Take Us?

In addition to the enormous current and near-future applications of CDT technology in healthcare, what lies ahead for the long term? One area very relevant to a world that is has been reeling from the effects of the global COVID-19 pandemic is public health.

If we have learned one lesson from the COVID-19 crisis, it is the strain the pandemic has put on hospitals and health resources. With the creation of a digital twin of a given hospital or specific departments within the hospital, resource management and planning can be viewed from a broad perspective in terms of more accurate management of resources so that allocation of critical resources such as ventilators or ICU beds can be better planned.

In a related aspect, the same way that we can envision individual cognitive digital twins to monitor our own personal health, we can use the individuals' digital twins to eventually create digital twins to model entire populations and run cases-based simulations, which, as you can imagine, could have enormous value to public health during another crisis similar to COVID-19.

This idea of a "Cognitive Digital Swarm" introduced in 2016 by Dr. Ahmed El Adl is being explored by the Department of Defense within different strategic initiatives. It looks into the idea of dynamically creating a digital swarm out of the individuals' twins related to an entire military unit or only a mission. Soldiers can transmit data to their digital twins from a distance by wearing clothing that is equipped with sensors without restricting their mobility.

The digital swarm would gather information from the entire unit and share relevant information back with the whole swarm, such as sharing ongoing mission real-time information or when soldiers may be injured and how to intervene. The same swarm concept can be used to create a team of relevant digital twins of the patient, medical doctors, medical equipment, and possibly drugs to predict health issues and proactively recommend preventive personalized healthcare services.

Before we get to large-scale population models, cognitive digital twins are already taking those first dramatic steps into creating the virtual self and the ultimate expression of personalized medicine. We opened this chapter with an understanding of how digital twins are being used in the mechanical world. The system being twinned, like an engine, is equipped with sensors that relay real-time status information to its digital twin that is analyzing the data in real time. It is thus able to get insights about its performance and predict when the object it is modeling needs maintenance. As such, operators don't need regular checkups of this particular engine but only intervene when indicated by the digital twin.

We already have many such sensors to monitor many vital parameters of the human body, and more are being developed daily. Fitbit and other specialized health trackers are already being combined with telemedicine apps and allowing doctors and individuals to make better-informed health decisions. It is not so much of a stretch to soon be able to use the data from such devices and other more specific sensors to link to 3D models of your organs. Wearable sensors will feed real-time data to remote servers that are continuously maintaining your digital twin. Both you and your doctors (or their digital twins) will receive regular notifications regarding specific tests, procedures, or even changes in lifestyle that need to be done as preventive measures—or receive an immediate alert if you are at risk of some kind of health crisis requiring intervention.

Most of the technologies needed to create useful cognitive digital twins in healthcare exist today, and it is already being used to a limited capacity. The challenge is for companies and institutions to start testing and applying this technology to specific healthcare problems. However, it is that very challenge that should be seen as a gauntlet tossed to start-ups considering venturing into providing AI-driven innovative solutions for healthcare.

As AI and CDT technology continues to improve, and with the anticipation of visionary start-ups based on same, the exponential increase in biological data acquisition, computing power, and AI modeling will not only deepen our understanding of how the human body functions, but it will also fulfill on the promise of personalized medicine, better and safer treatments of diseases, and the effective delivery of healthcare services.

TAKEAWAYS

- A digital twin is a computerized representation of a physical system that is augmented or enhanced by AI.

- Cognitive digital twins have been used for many years to model high-value mechanical systems, such as aircraft, ships, and vehicles. The technology is only just beginning to be used to model and simulate biological systems.

- Early successes in using CDT technology have been the development of virtual organs such as hearts and lungs. These types of virtual organs have created a new method of "in silico" research that may promise to forever change the landscape of medical research and drug discovery.

- AI and digital twins (of humans and machines) are revolutionizing the methods with which we acquire health data from patients, the precision and speed of medical imaging, as well as the high-precision automatic interpretation of images that exceeds the precision of human radiologists in a fraction of time and costs.

- The ultimate goal of cognitive digital twinning in healthcare will be the eventual development of personalized digital twins of individuals, ushering in an incredible era of personalized medicine for all.

That last bullet point and what we discussed in this chapter about personalized medicine will rely heavily on connectivity, which we will see in our next chapter on the Internet of Things.

CHAPTER 5

Internet of Things—IoT

We are all now connected by the Internet,
like neurons in a giant brain.

—STEPHEN HAWKING

The Internet of Things (IoT), sometimes also referred to as The Internet of Everything (IoE), is a term used to describe the network of physical objects that we know as the "smart things" that are embedded with sensors, software, and other technologies for the purpose of connecting and exchanging data with other devices and systems over the internet.

Entering the 2020 decade, more devices are connected to the internet than ever before, and this will continue to grow at a rapid trajectory. Worldwide, more than 21 billion devices have been estimated to be connected to the internet in 2020, which is five times the number of devices four years prior.[9]

These devices range from ordinary household objects to sophisticated industrial tools and, of course, medical devices.

In our last chapter, we learned of the value of sensors and how they have made digital twins possible. These kinds of sensors are everywhere. It is the dozens of sensors in cars that have made our CarTwin initiative possible. We have sensors in our home, such as on Ring cameras that can detect movement and Nest smart thermostats that can monitor and automatically adjust temperatures; IoT allows for the information from those sensors to be fed to your phone or to an Apple watch. Which is a good place to begin our discussion of IoT and healthcare because something like an Apple watch not only can monitor and process the information from the other interconnected devices, but it has built-in sensors itself that can monitor things like your pulse and heart rate. More on this later.

Sensors are everywhere; in fact, there are probably more of them in your phone than you use or care to realize! The thing about sensors that makes them such a key foundation is that AI and IoT have built upon is that the ubiquity of sensors has not only led to an explosion of data that can be exploited, but it also is good data; it is 100 percent accurate data, of course so long as the sensor is operating properly. But when you can feed massive amounts of good data into an AI engine, almost anything is possible.

All of these disparate kinds of data being fed into the cloud— video recordings, audio records, digital information from all sorts of monitoring sensors—creates a ripe environment for AI because that is exactly what AI does best. It takes huge data sets in any format and

---

9   Research Markets, "Internet of Things (IoT) in Healthcare," published 2019, https://www.medicaldevice-network.com/comment/bringing-internet-things-healthcare/.

can make sense of it and make extremely accurate predictions based upon that data.

The Internet of Things in Healthcare

In terms of healthcare, it can readily be seen how IoT allows for the interactivity between bedside monitors, smartwatches, fitness trackers, implanted medical devices, and any other "thing" that transmits or receives a signal containing pertinent medical data that can then be accessed or stored from or to anywhere.

In broad terms, IoT is changing the very nature of data acquisition and data analytics as they are applied to healthcare, transforming both into something far deeper and more powerful.

Traditionally, healthcare organizations currently base most of their clinical and financial analytics on conventional data sources like EHRs, insurance claims data, and lab results. But now, thanks to the Internet of Things, they are starting to integrate behavioral data from clients' credit cards or fitness data from health trackers and smartphone data, including searches for health topics and likes on social media.

> **In broad terms, IoT is changing the very nature of data acquisition and data analytics as they are applied to healthcare, transforming both into something far deeper and more powerful.**

Add to all of that things like remote monitoring from internet-connected prescription bottles, Bluetooth-connected scales, or blood glucose monitors—and IoT is bringing a vastness and richness of data to healthcare that was never before possible and can improve patient care across the board.

The focal point of AI and IoT applications are AI chips. Unlike the other chips you may be familiar with that are in your phone, computers, and other devices, AI chips are unique processors designed to allow the specialized processing of AI applications, sensing, and digital modeling. These AI chips are known by various names, but collectively they could be referred to as the AI processing unit (AI PU).

Until recently, all AI computations pretty much had to be performed remotely in data centers, on enterprise core appliances with large CPUs or GPUs, or on telecom edge processors, but there really was not a way to have the complexities of AI processing done on local or handheld devices. This is because AI computations are extremely processor-intensive, requiring hundreds of traditional chips of varying types to execute.

Today, AI chips are changing all that. They are physically smaller, relatively inexpensive, use much less power, and generate much less heat, making it possible to integrate them into handheld devices such as smartphones, Fitbits, etc. By enabling these devices to perform processor-intensive AI computations locally, AI chips have reduced or eliminated the need to send large data packets to a remote location that, combined with IoT and the ubiquity of WiFi, is the real game-changer.

Much of the AI applications we have discussed thus far rely on the power of AI chips integrated with IoT. It is AI chips that have allowed many AI-driven things that are already in practical use, such as being able to protect a system or area from security threats involving real-time facial recognition, chatbots for retail or businesses that interact with customers, and Natural Language Processing for voice assistants.

In healthcare, AI chips have allowed for an increase in patient-generated data of all shapes and sizes, which has led to applications such as prescription bottles that can automatically trigger medication refills, glucose monitors that can text message reminders to watch sugar intake, or wearable or implanted medical devices that can even trigger a call from a human healthcare coordinator when something seems off with a patient.

I recently had a remarkable opportunity to see how AI chips and the integration of IoT and healthcare when I was lucky enough to be invited to tour a Becton Dickinson facility.

Becton Dickinson is probably one of the most recognizable names there is in the medical device industry. You can barely walk the halls of any hospital without running into the "BD" logo on dozens of devices every few yards.

At the Becton Dickinson Experience Center in San Diego, it was mind-boggling to see how BD is integrating AI chips into their devices. They are already a company that, for years, has been making devices to monitor patients and collect data on patients and feed that to central databases, be that from devices in the ICU, ordinary hospital rooms, or wearable devices on mobile patients.

But what I got to see on this tour is that now, BD is incorporating AI chips into many of these devices so that not only can they monitor patients and relay information, they can use AI to make predictive and intuitive decisions or real-time alerts for patients.

It is really remarkable, because to the patient, you do not even know that these chips are there, but the machine learning and AI processing are now being built right into the medical devices themselves, be that an EKG monitor, oxygen sensor, what-have-you, it is now an integral part of the device.

What the tour had me realize is that AI and the Internet of Things are growing steadily for healthcare applications all around us, allowing healthcare providers to generate actionable insights on a scale and level of sophistication never possible before. To get an idea of the vastness of that scope, we can once again look at how AI, digital twinning, and IoT impact each of the stakeholders we have previously identified in healthcare delivery.

IoT and Patient Care

IoT and AI can enhance the delivery of healthcare to patients, providing better patient outcomes by proactively predicting health issues and the ability to diagnose, treat, and monitor patients both in and out of the hospital setting.

From the patient care perspective, IoT can be considered as any device that can collect health-related data from patients, including computing devices, mobile phones, smart bands and wearables, digital medications, implantable surgical devices, or other portable devices that can measure medical data and connect to the internet.

Again, the foundation of such devices is the integration of sensors and AI chips. These technologies allow for treatments to be monitored in real-time and facilitate the acquisition of vast amounts of physiological and clinical data about a patient so that diagnoses and high-quality treatment can be fast-tracked. There are many examples of how this is already being used.

One of our partners is a medical device company called Propeller Health, which has developed smart inhalers for the treatment of patients with COPD or asthma. It was a very simple yet elegant application of this technology. Basically, the inhaler can monitor how often it is being used, and under the circumstances it is being used so that the patient can better manage his or her symptoms as the device "learns" more about his or her usage.

The device itself can be attached to any inhaler the patient is already using. Once attached they simply keep using the inhaler as always. The sensors in the device automatically track where, when, and how often you use your medication, and they send that information to an app on your phone. Over time, the AI learns about your flare-ups and your medication usage and can help you become an expert at managing your symptoms and identifying your triggers.

It also creates reports and alerts that can be shared with your doctor so that he or she can better monitor your condition and modify your treatment plan as needed.

Another company we are working with is using AI and IoT to monitor and provide safety and security for Alzheimer's and dementia patients. This one is known as Kin-Keepers, and it is truly remarkable and leverages much of the technologies we have been talking about, including AI, IoT, and NLP—and it does this in the form of a virtual pet!

The smart pet, in the shape of a parrot, listens and learns the way a senior with dementia or other memory disorder speaks. This is a big problem with such patients; the disease causes a disconnect between the brain and verbal processing, so that the patient may be thinking and saying, "I need to use the toilet," but what comes out of their mouth is really "Can I have a candy bar?" However, the parrot, using integrated AI chips, learns the language of the senior over time and gives them the voice and understanding that they otherwise would not have.

Additionally, the smart pets, which the company calls "Assistive Selves," listen remotely and can alert families to loneliness, abuse, neglect, or just plain sadness. Furthermore, by leveraging IoT—the "parrots" can be connected with other parrots around the world, which means that people with Alzheimer's or dementia never need to be alone, and even with cognitive impairment, new friendships can be born. And once interconnected thusly, connected Assistive Selves learn from each other—how to be better, smarter pets for their owners and families.

These are only a few examples of how AI chips and IoT are changing the very nature of patient care. Every day, we are seeing expanded use of smart devices incorporating sensors and AI chips that allow remote review, care, and monitoring of patients whether in the hospital or in their own homes, which is creating a new continuum of care through the Internet of Things.

In fact, Google recently unveiled plans to produce a specialized line of AI chips, circuit boards, and cameras designed specifically to run AI programs locally and within a mass-produced product whose first applications out of beta testing were both in healthcare.

One is an Orlando-based company that is using Google's hardware to develop an autonomous monitoring platform that helps detect patient falls and other dangers. According to the company care. ai, "by employing cameras and computer vision analysis, the onboard AI is designed to interpret the data on its own and notify caregivers of any potential situations. This can include whether someone is at risk for developing pressure ulcers in a hospital bed or if a person with dementia leaves their room or another area. The wall-mounted system is designed to have no burden on patients with no wearable devices while lessening the workload and attention required by staff or caregivers in both home and hospital settings."

The other is San Francisco-based Virgo Surgical Video Solutions which aims to enlist Google's AI chips to quickly spot polyps and potential cases of colon cancer. While the company does not yet have a timeline for clinical trials of the device, a demo in a simulated colon showed how the system outlines and highlights polyps whenever they're in view of the endoscope in real-time.

The combination of AI and IoT is providing a great opportunity to proactively predict health issues and diagnose, treat, and monitor patients both in and out of the hospital, but that is hardly the only place where they are making a huge impact in healthcare.

The Impact of IoT on Research Drug Discovery

As you might imagine, IoT has immense power to revolutionize pharmaceutical manufacturing in processes, particularly in drug discovery, where IoT allows researchers remote patient access and AI/CDT-driven patient monitoring.

As we have pointed out in previous chapters, the process of drug discovery takes massive amounts of time and money. Already some of the top pharma companies from around the world are adopting IoT technologies in their discovery and manufacturing operations to improve efficiency and speed to market.

As we discussed in Chapter 4, in silico—"organs on a chip"—research is revolutionizing drug discovery.

When combined with IoT applications, in silico research can increase the odds of finding a winning drug formulation from dozens of combinations tested against a specifically targeted virtual organ like a heart or a lung.

As opposed to traditional drug discovery, an in silico drug trial not only enables an experiment but also communicates the outcome of what happened in the chip after the test of the given therapeutic compound.

Another remarkable advantage of leveraging IoT technology with in silico drug trials is that since the trial participant cannot be monitored remotely going about their everyday lives, researchers can get massive data on how lifestyle may impact the effectiveness of the particular drug they are testing. For example, what is the impact of the amount of sleep a patient is getting on the drug's therapeutic value, or exercise, or lack of same? How is their diet affecting the outcome of the trial? Any behavior that the scientists wish to account for can now easily be incorporated into the trial.

IoT also eases the administration of clinical trials because now trial participants can be tracked and monitored anywhere and are not restricted to getting the trial medications tested only at the research center or hospital running the trial. Not only does IoT lift the obligation for on-site treatments and frequent check-ins, but it also broadens the pool of eligible individuals to those who may not have the ability to travel great distances.

In a nutshell, the benefits of IoT for clinical trials include the following:

- Increased patient engagement and empowerment

- Much more flexible trial design

- More efficient patient enrollment and retention

- Richer, higher quality data and integrity

- Real-time data capture from anywhere

- Reduced operational expenses and remote patient monitoring

In addition to research and drug discovery, pharma is also using IoT technologies for manufacturing and supply chain. In a manufacturing plant, with IoT monitoring sensors, drugmakers can instantaneously feed all relevant facility data into a single dashboard and can alert a supervisor in case of any abnormal conditions or urgent maintenance requirements. As in any digital twin/IoT manufacturing, IoT in pharmaceutical manufacturing also enables handling alerts and any critical conditions in machinery remotely.

As for supply chain, once drugs leave the manufacturing facility, they have to travel through different modes of transport and may be subject to varying temperatures and weather conditions. Although in most cases, care is undertaken to maintain the packages within the prescribed temperatures, chances of variations during transit cannot be completely ruled out. IoT can be helpful in such situations to provide real-time data to manufacturers with improved supply chain visibility. This was especially relevant during the transport of the recently developed coronavirus vaccines that had to be maintained at very specific temperatures across the supply chain.

IoT and Medication Compliance

Another area where IoT and AI is making a big difference related to drugs but not necessarily in discovery or delivery is in medication compliance. Medication compliance is a real problem, particularly with elderly patients who forget to take medications or to reorder prescriptions when needed.

It has been estimated that at least 125,000 deaths per year[10] in the U.S. are attributed to non-adherence of medication, and 33 to 69 percent[11] of medication-related hospital admissions are due to poor drug compliance. Beyond distressing statistics like

---

10   R. McCarthy, "The Price You Pay for the Drug Not Taken," *Business Health*, 16 (October 16, 1998): 27–33, https://pubmed.ncbi.nlm.nih.gov/10185113/.

11   Lars Osterberg and Terrence Blaschke, "Adherence to Medication," *The New England Journal of Medicine*, 353 (August 4, 2005): 487–97, https://pubmed.ncbi.nlm.nih.gov/16079372/.

those—drug noncompliance or poor adherence has personal and societal costs, including poor health outcomes leading to increased morbidity and mortality, lost productivity, and compromised quality of life. AI chip-driven IoT-enabled devices have a role to play in drug compliance through smart devices that provide reminders to the patient, notifications to providers and remote medication adherence monitoring. Some of these examples we have already discussed, such as Propeller's inhalers, other examples include smart pill bottles and smart pill dispensers that can enable better connections between patients and caregivers. They can remind patients to take their medications and alert caregivers when prescriptions are taken or missed.

IoT and Hospital Administration

The IoT has opened a world of possibilities for hospital administration. Of course, the kind of data that the facility receives from the monitors already discussed streamline many processes from billing to intake and release of patients. But beyond direct connectivity to patients, IoT can improve healthcare delivery and streamline hospital operations in many other ways. A primary example is in resource allocation and inventory control.

AI and IoT applications are being leveraged to help reduce the time spent seeking or tracking medications and high-value medical equipment, freeing up more time for providers to dedicate to patient treatment. The information these AI-enabled devices provide can be used to inform better resource allocation decisions.

We worked with a partner in developing such an application to track and monitor the use of portable x-ray machines.

Basically, what they did was put the sensor on the machines so they could track them from a resource utilization perspective. The hospital administrator can now literally track on a real-time map exactly where that x-ray machine or any device equipped with the sensor is at any given moment in time on an iPad or smartphone. Let's say you have ten or twenty of these machines in use throughout the hospital, and you need to disperse one quickly to any location in the hospital; you can instantly see where the closest available machine is.

The person responsible for resource allocation can literally see on a master control system what machines are being used and where, and you can know at a moment's notice if you are getting dangerously close to a shortage of some critical devices and plan accordingly. You can see how something like this could really have saved lives during the COVID pandemic when there was and continues to be shortages of ICU beds and ventilators.

In addition, the sensors also help prevent theft, generate insights on the utilization of medical devices, including conditions that result in malfunction, and can alert hospital administrators when devices may need maintenance.

Where Can This Take Us?

There can be no doubt that Big Data, AI, and the Internet of Things have become major players in healthcare.

As far as where can IoT take us, unlike some of the other concepts we have been discussing thus far that are only in their infancy at best, IoT is already here in a big way. The number of IoT devices worldwide is forecast to almost triple from 8.74 billion in 2020 to more than 25.4 billion IoT devices in 2030.[12]

The future will likely bring us a world where AI and IoT applications will assist all and even take over some of the tasks currently executed by healthcare providers, researchers, and facility administrators.

> **Once AI-chip/IoT-based medical technology can deliver on all its promises, the healthcare industry can streamline research, enhance patient care, ensure better treatment compliance, and improve the allocation of critical resources, all while cutting costs dramatically.**

Many believe that IoT in healthcare has the potential to improve overall population health and transition our healthcare system to a true model of primary, secondary, and tertiary care, where the health system can use its existing workforce and infrastructure in new and more efficient ways.

When fully implemented, AI-driven IoT can eliminate the risk of human error in diagnoses and offer reliable, accurate information for expedited care and treatments. It can also improve the clinical workflow and free up time for doctors and physicians to interact with and consult with their patients, lessening the amount of time patients would have to wait for treatment.

Once AI-chip/IoT-based medical technology can deliver on all its promises, the healthcare industry can streamline research, enhance patient care, ensure better treatment compliance, and improve the allocation of critical resources, all while cutting costs dramatically.

---

12   Lionel Sujay Vailshery, "Number of IoT connected devices worldwide 2019-2021, with forecasts to 2030," statista.com, published November 22, 2022, https://www.statista.com/statistics/1183457/iot-connected-devices-worldwide/.

TAKEAWAYS

- The combination of AI chips and the Internet of Things is already making tremendous changes in healthcare delivery.

- AI and IoT is being used extensively for patient care and monitoring.

- AI and IoT is streamlining drug discovery and pharmaceutical manufacturing and is improving pharma supply chain and logistics.

- AI and IoT has value in resource allocation and inventory tracking.

There are still some hurdles to be faced before there can be full-scale and ubiquitous adoption of IoT applications for healthcare, not the least of which are potential security, bias, and privacy concerns, all of which will be discussed in our next chapter.

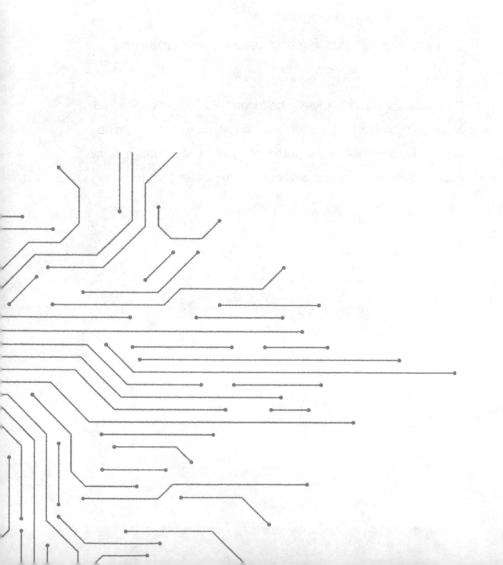

Testing AI Applications and Addressing Bias

Artificial intelligence is just a new tool, one that can be used for good and for bad purposes and one that comes with new dangers and downsides as well.

—SARAH JEONG

Anyone who has ever been involved in developing any kind of enterprise software application knows that it takes a lot more in the developmental stages than merely putting the code strings together, and then boom— you are ready for market. It takes testing, testing, and then some more testing to make sure it works before delivery. And even then, despite your best Quality Assurance (QA) efforts, any IT professional will tell you that there still will be plenty of bugs on arrival.

QA is such a core part of any technology delivery that it's one of the most essential components of any project development methodology. Yet, there are those that have said that since we cannot apply traditional methods of QA testing for AI applications, we cannot avoid inherent bias and other problems that can get inadvertently "embedded" in the programs and that it is this challenge that is standing in the way of the large-scale adoption of AI, particularly in healthcare.

Human biases affecting data acquisition and analysis have been well-documented. Known biases and those that we may not even be aware of have been known to throw off experiments and research and affect outcomes in undesirable ways. The very nature of the scientific method has "objectivity" at its core for a reason, and the researcher, the problem solver, or the truth seeker, wants to avoid any kind of bias as much as possible. However, there are some intrinsic human biases that can worm their way into any project simply because they are ingrained in human nature.

As AI is beginning to permeate so much of lives, as we saw when discussing IoT in the last chapter, there is a growing concern about the extent to which these human biases can weave their way into artificial intelligence systems with potentially dreadful results. At a time when so many industries are looking to deploy AI systems across their operations, being acutely aware of those risks and working to reduce them is an urgent priority. Nowhere is this more urgent than in healthcare, where intrinsic bias could impact patient outcomes.

However, addressing bias is a challenge that AI developers and would-be AI start-ups are well aware of and are taking steps to invent new models and new QA testing methodologies specific to AI and, in particular, to weed out any potential of "built-in" biases upfront before the applications get put into general use.

What exactly do we mean by bias in AI or so-called "algorithmic bias"? There have been some very high-profile cases of "algorithmic bias" in the news lately. It can be something as simple as an AI-driven speech recognition program being able to identify the pronoun "his" but unable to identify "hers," or more insidious examples such as facial recognition software that has been deployed that is less likely to recognize people of color. While entirely eliminating bias in AI is not possible, it's essential that those considering start-ups in AI—especially in developing AI for healthcare applications—know not only how to reduce bias in AI but actively work to prevent it.

Bias Creep

How does bias creep its way into AI algorithms in the first place?

Bias can worm its way into AI algorithms in several ways. AI systems learn to make decisions based on training data. Unfortunately, that data can already be tainted with previously biased human decision making or generally reflective of unfortunate historical, social inequities. That can happen even when the developer takes pains to remove sensitive variables such as gender, race, or sexual orientation. For example. Amazon had to stop using a hiring algorithm after finding it favored applicants based on words like "executed" or "captured" that were more commonly found

The goal of eliminating bias in AI models is to ensure that the algorithm in question has equal predictive value across disparate groups or to make sure that models have equal false positive and false negative rates across groups.

on men's resumes.[13] Another source of bias is flawed data sampling, in which groups are over or underrepresented in the training data. For example, Joy Buolamwini at MIT, working with Timnit Gebru, found that facial analysis technologies had higher error rates for minorities and particularly minority women, potentially due to unrepresentative training data.[14]

The goal of eliminating bias in AI models is to ensure that the algorithm in question has equal predictive value across disparate groups or to make sure that models have equal false positive and false negative rates across groups.

The Real-Time Feedback Loop

One of the best ways we have found to eliminate errors and bias in the development of AI algorithms is to use what I call a "real-time feedback loop"; others have called this "reinforcement learning." Remember, the whole foundation of AI is that these programs can learn, so reinforcement learning or real-time feedback is a way to train the AI to weed out bias or any other negative behavior of the program before it is implemented.

It involves a kind of trial-and-error learning, the same way that you might train a child or a puppy. Real-time feedback or reinforcement learning has proven to be very successful for AI and robotics.

Basically, much as you would do when training a puppy, you reward your AI algorithm for "good behavior" or the things it gets right as it tries different actions and different solutions and "punish

---

13   James Manyika, Jake Silberg, and Brittany Presten, "What Do We Do About the Biases in AI," *Harvard Business Review*, published October 25, 2019, https://hbr.org/2019/10/what-do-we-do-about-the-biases-in-ai.

14   Ibid.

it" for when its approach fails at a task. Over time, it begins to figure out which actions in which situations lead to the most reward. The way to implement this positive feedback loop in training AI is with a concept known as the "Red Button."

The real-time feedback loop accounts for the fact that AI models are not static. Just like the human intelligences they model, they change and grow through their entire lifetime. A common but major mistake many AI start-ups make is deploying their model without a way for end-users to give them real-time feedback on how the model is making its decisions and predictions in the real world. Creating a methodology for real-time feedback can ensure that your model is maintaining optimal performance levels for every person, group, or demographic.

The Red Button

The "red button" in AI development is a way for a human to intervene when the algorithm is doing something you do not want it to do. To, in effect, hit a virtual red *Stop* button, so the AI gets a clear message that what it is doing is wrong.

It gives you an opportunity to change course, modify data sets, and adjust the bias out of the program before something harmful gets embedded in the system. Anytime the human investigator wants to interrupt the task the AI is working on or the prediction it is making, for whatever reason, the operator "pushes the red button." Over time, the same way that a mouse can be trained to avoid doing certain behaviors with a mild electric shock, the AI begins to see the red button as a punishment, and it will, over time, learn to only perform a sequence of actions that prevent the button from ever being pressed.

Other Methods of Reducing Bias

Another key component to avoid introducing bias into your AI algorithms is to have diversity on your development team. We have made this a major priority at our companies and joint ventures. Each of us brings different experiences and ideas to the development project. People from diverse backgrounds—race, gender, age, experience, culture, etc.—will inherently ask different questions and interact with your model in different ways. That can help you catch problems with bias before your model is in production.

Ultimately to avoid human bias in the development of AI algorithms, it all comes down to the old axiom that every computer programmer knows—"garbage in, garbage out." In other words, every computer program—even with programming as sophisticated as AI—is only as good as the programming and quality assurance testing behind it.

Explainable AI

These questions about testing and bias in AI systems are all part of the broader question: "How can we trust AI?" This is a very important question, particularly as AI becomes more ubiquitous, thanks to integration with IoT, and in light of the fact that biases in decision-making algorithms used by some insurance and healthcare companies have become apparent.

The answer seems to be a new development in the AI arena that is directly targeting this problem known as "explainable AI," or XAI. Explainable AI is a set of processes and modeling, methods that are designed to help the ultimate end-user of your AI application better comprehend and trust the results created by your ML algorithm.

How does an AI arrive at a decision or prediction it makes?

The immensely complicated digital reasoning that an AI algorithm uses to come up with its results is almost impossible to backtrack and understand exactly how the algorithm came to the conclusion that it did. So engineers have to refer to the process as a "black box" or "black box learning."

These black box models are created directly from the data, and the algorithms drill down into that data in such a deep and complex way that not even we who create the programs can ever truly understand or explain what exactly is happening inside them or how the AI algorithm arrived at a specific result. Hence, we just call it a "black box" for something mysterious and unknown.

Basically, black box or traditional AI outputs a prediction, but it doesn't tell you how it got there; it just says, "trust me, it's right because I am the AI, and you are not." Because no one can peer into the "black box," often, companies don't find out that their AI is biased until it's too late.

Explainable AI, which is also being called "white box AI" as opposed to black box, is a set of tools, techniques, and models intended to help both end-users and designers of an AI algorithm to better understand their predictions, including how and why the systems arrived at its conclusions. Basically, white box AI or explainable AI makes all decision-relevant factors visible and therefore brings an inherent bias bubbling to the surface.

Basically, white box AI or explainable AI makes all decision-relevant factors visible and therefore brings an inherent bias bubbling to the surface.

A good example of a recent XAI start-up is Fiddler Labs, based in San Francisco and founded by ex-Facebook and Samsung engineers. As co-founder and CPO Amit Paka told *Forbes* magazine, its software makes the behavior of AI models transparent and understandable.

This is extremely important in the context of bias and the ethics of AI. XAI enables operations, like a hospital, for example, to identify potential discrimination against certain groups and demographics. But, most importantly, it will enable them to correct their AI models before they're deployed at scale, thereby avoiding scandal-ridden headlines.

XAI will be critical for combating algorithmic bias as more AI apps make their way into the healthcare field. We know that gender, race, and other demographic categories might not be explicitly encoded in algorithms, but XAI can help facilities discover the sometimes subtle and deep biases that can creep inadvertently into data that is fed into these complex algorithms.

Making AI models more transparent through explainable AI can be key to overcoming many of the factors that inadvertently lead to bias. There are many start-ups right now that are strictly focused on the development of and deployment of XAI solutions.

Where Can This Take Us?

Because AI algorithms are meant to make predictions and decisions based on interpretations of huge data sets, they're often thought to be unbiased. However, as sophisticated as these machine learning models are, they are still programmed by humans with their own intrinsic biases and trained on socially generated data. This poses the challenge and risk of introducing and amplifying existing human biases into models, preventing AI from truly working for everyone.

If we are to ever fulfill on the promise of the future of AI in healthcare, we must make every effort to ensure that it works the same way for every patient without bias or unintentional malice.

TAKEAWAYS

- Because AI algorithms are created by humans, there is always the possibility of human biases creeping into the applications.

- Real-time testing and obtaining real-time and real-world feedback are basic ways to avoid bias in AI.

- Diversity of development teams is a very good way to avoid bias in the rollout of AI solutions.

- Explainable AI is a next-generation AI development solution that specifically targets and is designed to eliminate bias in AI systems before they are deployed.

In our next chapter, we will take our deepest dive yet into the state-of-the-art and the bright future for AI and drug discovery.

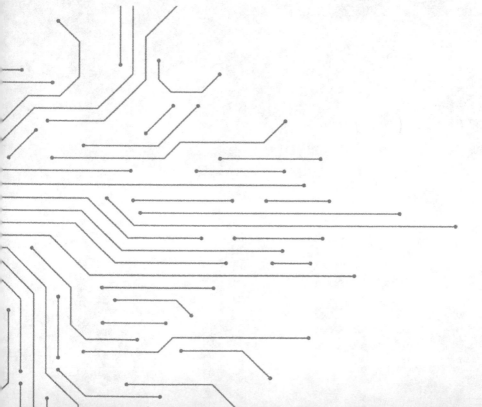

AI and Drug Discovery

*All you need is lots and lots of data and lots of information
about what the right answer is, and you'll be able
to train a big neural net to do what you want.*

—GEOFFREY HINTON

As you may have gleaned from the previous chapters, perhaps the greatest impact and opportunities for AI in healthcare are in the arena of drug discovery.

Traditional drug discovery is an extremely long, complicated, and expensive process. There are basically four phases of drug discovery— early drug discovery, preclinical phase, the clinical phases, and regulatory approval. Most people are familiar with the clinical phases, which itself has four phases of trials, Phases 1, 2, 3, and 4.

It can take up to ten years on average for a drug to go through the entire process of all of the phases from early discovery, through the clinical trials up through FDA approval, and eventually into the marketplace. Over those ten years, you are also looking at an expenditure of about $5 billion.

Why is it so expensive, and why does it take so long to develop a new drug?

The simplest answer is because, at the core of traditional drug discovery, most current methodologies are not very good at making predictions. And predictions are the very basis of biopharmaceutical research. We need to predict what a new molecule will do to a specified target in a patient.

As surely you have come to learn by now, AI is all about making better predictions, and this is exactly why AI is already and will play a much more critical role in the future in drug discovery and development, in particular, making the entire process shorter and much more cost-efficient.

Only about 10 percent of all drugs that start in early drug discovery make it through the entire process. A drug can fail at any point in the process. The later it fails, obviously, the more costly it is in terms of time and money. This is what makes AI so attractive for drug discovery and pharma research. AI streamlines and makes each of the phases more efficient. In doing so, it not only helps get more successful drugs to market that much sooner, but it also helps to weed out unsuccessful drugs much earlier in the process, saving a lot of wasted time and money.

AI streamlines and accelerates the entire process of drug discovery, making every phase more efficient. This has been dramatically demonstrated by a company known as Insilico Medicine. Insilico developed an AI software specifically for drug discovery and the pharmaceutical industry. By leveraging all of the AI technologies that we have discussed in our previous chapters, such as Natural Language Processing, advanced computing, digital twinning, and the inherent ability of AI to make predictions based on enormous data sets, Insilco has demonstrated an end-to-end process that reduced the typical ten year, $5 billion drug discovery model down to eighteen months and a cost of just $2.6 million. A remarkable reduction in time and money!

Insilico has already developed a groundbreaking proprietary AI-driven platform that effectively addresses the challenges of identifying accurate targets in the preclinical phase and develops novel molecular structures with desired parameters and predicts clinical trial outcomes in the later phases of drug discovery. In 2021, Insilico initiated the first-in-human study of a potentially first-in-class drug candidate with a novel target for fibrosis. Using its AI platform, the company completed the entire discovery process from target discovery to preclinical candidate nomination within eighteen months on a budget of $2.6 million. Furthermore, Insilico nominated two preclinical candidates with a novel molecular structure for anemia of chronic kidney disease and inflammatory bowel disease within twelve months using its AI engine.

There have already been several real-world examples of how AI is having a totally transformative effect on all the key steps of clinical trial design, from study preparation to execution to improving trial success rates, thus lowering the pharma research and development burden and at the same time making a positive impact on public health as new therapeutics make it to market faster.

If we pull apart Insilico's successful eighteen-month fibrosis trial, we can see how their AI solution leveraged each of the technologies and techniques that we have discussed in previous chapters and applied them in such a way as to accelerate every one of the four phases of drug discovery.

AI Drug Discovery and Natural Language Processing

As we have already learned, NLP is that aspect of AI which allows machine intelligence to better understand and interpret human language.

NLP plays an extremely vital role throughout each phase of leveraging AI for drug discovery, but where it is of particular value is in the early phase—the preclinical phase—when it comes to trail matching.

Machine learning, when leveraging NLP in particular, is able to automatically find patterns of meaning in large datasets such as text, speech, or images. NLP can understand and correlate content in written or spoken language, and human-machine interfaces allow for the more natural exchange of information between computers and humans.

We live in a world of amazing drug discovery. But for every effective drug or treatment that makes it through the rigors of clinical trials and eventually into the hands of doctors or pharmacists, there are hundreds and hundreds more that fail. You may not realize it, but most drug trials fail in their earliest stages.

Drug trials fail in the early stages for various reasons, but two of the main ones that have been identified by pharmaceutical researchers are suboptimal patient selection and recruiting techniques combined with the inability to monitor and coach patients effectively during clinical trials.[15]

These are two of the very things that NLP and AI can substantially improve.

NLP allows an AI algorithm that is seeking to find the most ideal candidates for a clinical drug trial by scouring through massive piles of data that is in disparate forms, ranging from the sophisticated language of peer-reviewed medical journals to the "legal-ese" language of insurance claim documents and EHRs, to the casual language of handwritten doctors' notes, and find the commonalities of the target patients the researcher is looking for.

Starting a drug trial in the earliest phases with better candidates raises the chances of success manyfold. As mentioned earlier, clinical trials take anywhere from ten to fifteen years and can consume $1.5–$2 billion if it goes to successful completion. A failed trial sinks not only the investment into the trial itself but also the preclinical development costs, rendering the loss per failed clinical trial at $800 million to $1.4 billion.[16]

Two of the key factors causing a clinical trial to fail that have been identified as unsuccessful are patient candidate selection and recruiting mechanisms, which fail to bring the best-suited patients to a trial in time, as well as the absence of reliable and efficient adherence control, patient monitoring, and clinical endpoint detection systems.

AI, as evidenced by the in silico trials and others, has been shown to help overcome these two major shortcomings of current early clinical trial design. Machine learning, when leveraging NLP in

---

15   Stefan Harrer, Pratik Shah, Bhavna Antony, and Jianying Hu, "Artificial Intelligence for Clinical Trial Design," *Trends in Pharmacological Sciences*, 40, no. 8 (2019): 577–591, https://pubmed.ncbi.nlm.nih.gov/31326235/.

16   Ibid

particular, is able to automatically find patterns of meaning in large datasets such as text, speech, or images. NLP can understand and correlate content in written or spoken language, and human-machine interfaces allow for the more natural exchange of information between computers and humans.

These capabilities can be used for correlating large and diverse datasets such as electronic health records (EHRs), medical literature, and trial databases for improved patient-trial matching and recruitment before a trial starts, as well as for monitoring patients automatically and continuously during the trial, thereby allowing improved adherence control and yielding more reliable and efficient endpoint assessment.

Beyond better trial matching in the early phase, which means a better chance of a successful trial, NLP has great benefit across the entire drug discovery process because of its clear ability to speed up and reduce errors in data analysis and development pipelines.

NLP algorithms can assist in the later stages of the drug discovery pipeline, from analyzing clinical trial digital pathology data to identifying predictive biomarkers and categorizing results.

For example, a key area that has been identified for success in the later phases of drug discovery is the effective and accurate identification of biomarkers. Biomarkers are now an essential part of the drug discovery process. A recent study by AstraZeneca[17] found that

- Eighty-two percent of projects were active or successful in Phase 2 when they included efficacy biomarkers, compared to 30 percent of projects without biomarkers.

---

17 David Cook, Dearg Brown, Robert Alexander, and et al., "Lessons Learned from the Fate of AstraZeneca's Drug Pipeline: A Five-dimensional Framework," *Nature Reviews Drug Discovery*, 13, (2014): 419–431, https://doi.org/10.1038/nrd4309.

- Safety and PK/PD biomarkers are critical to successful projects.

- Clinical biomarkers should be an "integral part of the R&D program" and used to guide patient selection "as early as possible."

Biomarkers can be defined as naturally occurring molecules, genes, or characteristics by which a particular pathological or physiological process, disease, etc. can be identified. There are two major types of biomarkers: biomarkers of exposure, which are used in risk prediction and safety/toxicity assessment, and biomarkers of disease, which are used in screening, diagnosis, and monitoring of disease progression.

These biomarkers can take different forms (e.g., enzymes) with varying activity, changes in expression levels of particular genes, or the presence or absence of individual metabolites. Linguamatics, an already well-established company developing AI solutions for healthcare and biotechnology companies, has developed an NLP-based AI algorithm for text mining, which has demonstrated a high success rate for identifying biomarkers.

The flexibility of Linguamatics NLP allows the user to search for any of these data types and to find relationships between known or novel markers and diseases, mutations, drugs, and more.

Linguamatics NLP platform allows researchers to identify targets in disease areas of interest and establish a ranking based on factors such as safety and potential for therapeutic benefit. According to the company, researchers at Merck used Linguamatics NLP and other tools to discover potential novel biomarkers and phenotypes for diabetes and obesity from PubMed, clinical trial data, and internal[18] Merck research documents.

At my company, BigRio, we have recently partnered with Eric Siegel. Eric has an extensive background in AI with a particular focus on molecular biology and drug discovery. He is proving to be an invaluable member of our team. Eric has said:

> Leveraging AI and NLP to speed up the overall process of drug discovery is one thing. But reducing the failures or increasing your likelihood of success is the other really key thing. Overall, when you use AI to achieve more successful pharma research and development, it has overarching effects for generations to come because you no longer are wasting millions and millions of dollars on failed trials. Instead, that money can go to investment in the right projects, better projects, and that can lead to the discovery of that one drug that saves the life of your kids or your grandkids.

Eric is now the CEO of our partner venture Citadel Discovery (www.citadeldiscovery.io). Citadel is focused on data and AI for early small molecule therapeutic (think: aspirin) drug discovery. The process of finding novel chemical material that can lead to candidates and ultimately drugs has been an expensive process, often heavily dependent on serendipity or extremely expensive molecule collections and infrastructure only available to Big Pharma. Our approach using DELs capitalizes on vast improvements in economics of generating

---

18   Linguamatics, "Text Analytics and natural language Processing in Drug Discovery," linguamatics.com, accessed March 11, 2022, https://www.linguamatics.com/solutions/drug-discovery.

highly information-rich data and the predictive models that can be built. By generating this data across hundreds to thousands of disease-relevant proteins from the human proteome and from relevant viral and bacterial sources, we are building a database that can be used to deeply characterize biological pathways, target classes and ultimately, as the data set scales, to explore the complex network of interactions between these proteins.

AI Drug Discovery and Quantum Computing

When you understand the sheer volume of data involved in drug discovery, obviously it is clear that quantum computing is already playing a major role and will continue to do so. This is particularly helpful in those earliest stages of drug discovery, where the enormous power of AI driven by quantum computers can be leveraged to identify drug targets more quickly and easily on the molecular level. Again, Insilico's proprietary AI, known as PandaOmics, did exactly this.

Developing molecular drug targets relies on something the industry calls "OMICS." OMICS is a term that applies to the analysis of large amounts of data representing an entire set of some kind, especially the entire set of molecules, such as proteins, lipids, or metabolites, in a cell, organ, or organism.

The term is derived from recent technical advances in gene sequencing, microarray, and mass spectrometry (MS) technologies that allow scientists to generate genomics, transcriptomics, proteomics, and other -omic data types at an unprecedented level of resolution and sophistication. The resulting super data-rich information can be utilized to identify drug targets, to uncover the mechanism of action of drugs, and to assess (or infer) their side effects. OMICS-based studies can also provide essential information to deliver personalized medicine. While traditional drug discovery can make use of OMICS, the sheer mass of OMICS datasets requires AI to leverage them for the greatest effect and impact.

According to Insilico, PandaOmics allows the researcher to access the full set of OMICS data generated by the scientific community so far. You do not need to spend your time trying to convert your data into an interpretable format or wait for a bioinformatician to do that for you—instead, you will find all the data already processed and uploaded in a uniform way, so you can focus on science and data interpretation. Furthermore, PandaOmics converts a list of seemingly unrelated genes into a connected story based on dysregulated molecular processes. PandaOmics uses a proprietary pathway analysis approach called iPanda to infer pathway activation or inhibition.

Quantum computing's ability to simulate larger, more complex molecules and OMICS datasets could be game-changing.

By leveraging the enormity of the genealogical DNA-targeted database, artificial intelligence algorithms within PandaOmics predict the chances of a potential target to enter Phase 1 of clinical trials for any disease in the next five years and estimate the chance of a successful phase-to-phase transition for disease-specific trials.

And right now, the software is accomplishing this at the cutting edge of conventional computing. When OMICS analysis tools like this can be coupled with quantum computers, as we discussed in Chapter 3, the potential is mind-boggling.

Quantum computing's ability to simulate larger, more complex molecules and OMICS datasets could be game-changing.

As we have discussed thus far, the development of molecular formulations that become drugs to treat or cure diseases is at the heart of drug discovery. In constantly seeking to improve the drug discovery process, pharma companies have for decades been early adopters of computational chemistry's digital tools, such as molecular dynamics (MD) simulations and density functional theory (DFT). As we have thus far explored and seen in the practical sense, recent drug discovery and development have taken advantage of AI. The next digital frontier for pharma is and will be quantum computing (QC).

Given its focus on molecular formations, drug discovery is a natural candidate for quantum computing. At their core, molecules—including those that might be used for drugs—are basically quantum systems subject to quantum dynamics. As we discussed in our chapter on quantum computing, QC, when combined with AI, is able to predict and simulate the structure, properties, behavior, and reactivity of these molecules more effectively than conventional computing can.

Model-exact molecular behaviors are computationally difficult for standard computers, and approximate methods are often not sufficiently accurate when interactions on the atomic level are critical, as is the case for finding suitable OMICS-based drug targets. Theoretically, quantum computers have the capacity to efficiently simulate the complete problem, including interactions on the atomic level. As these quantum computers become more powerful, tremendously accurate molecular modeling will become a reality and thus increase the speed and efficiency of drug discovery by a whole other order of magnitude.

Says Eric Siegel:

Right now, the only limit on the number of molecules that can be tested as targets is the limit of the computing power. How do I know that I have tested the right amount of targets? If I test 60 and do not find what I was looking for, should I have tested 100, 200? Conventional computers right now limit the number of and the accuracy of those models. But with quantum, the molecular models are not only more accurate, but they also are scalable; 1000, 100,000 are all possible and all almost instantaneously when you are dealing with the processing power of thousand cubits that you have with quantum computing.

AI Drug Discovery and Cognitive Digital Twins

In Chapter 4, we already demonstrated how cognitive digital twins have changed the very nature of pharma research and drug discovery. In fact, the company Insilico took its name from the new paradigm of "in silico" research that AI and CDT technology created.

As we discussed at length in that chapter, this kind of in silico research, made possible by digital twin technology, is already changing the landscape of drug research and discovery.

Again, just as with NLP, CDT speeds up drug discovery, but now more in the clinical phases because of the fact that now researchers can test the drugs in an extraordinarily accurate but virtual setting rather than a real setting.

So now, instead of all the difficulties discussed in having to find "real" patients, you can simulate the effects of a therapeutic on a virtual lung, virtual heart, etc. These digital twins are increasingly getting better at representing the mechanism of action of a therapy. Digital twins of patients are growing in sophistication as more longitudinal biomarker data becomes available, and as discussed in Chapter 6, it is only a matter of time until we can leverage all that data to develop entire digital twins of real people.

The use of properly configured digital twins also helps to ensure experiments are of constant quality and meet industry QC standards, so twins can assist after trial and approval in manufacturing and help to take a developmental drug to scale.

We have already cited several examples of how digital twins and "organs on a chip" are already being effectively used to hasten drug discovery and provide for more efficient clinical trials, and I refer the reader back to the work of Dr. Kaul and the others we discussed in that chapter.

But to sum it up, for the sake of this discussion, the benefits of using digital twins in drug discovery go beyond simply the reductions in experimentation time and waste. The use of properly configured digital twins also helps to ensure experiments are of constant quality and meet industry QC standards, so twins can assist after trial and approval in manufacturing and help to take a developmental drug to scale.

But that's only the beginning. As human digital twins become more advanced, researchers can use an interface and the simulation model of the "virtual patient" to simulate lifestyle treatment outcomes, for example, how diet or exercise may affect the patient's outcomes.

CDTs can also be used to create patient engagement materials to help them better manage the condition and researchers to ensure better monitoring and compliance during the trials.

Another thing about CDT in drug discovery that we did not touch upon in that earlier chapter that is worth noting is that CDTs could eventually totally eliminate the controversial use of animal subjects in drug testing. Digital twins can be configured to simulate the environment in which a drug or medical device will be used and run it through all of its paces and perimeters, which means the twin could replace many of the bench and animal tests currently done.

Drug Discovery and the Internet of Things

As discussed, on average, one winning solution out of nine promising drug formulations makes it through the drug discovery process. Just as the other aspects of AI, the Internet of Things (IoT) is already playing a significant role in accelerating drug development, streamlining all of the four phases, lowering the discovery costs, as well as improving the administration of medicine to patients.

IoT is best leveraged in drug discovery when coupled with the cognitive digital twins of the aforementioned in silica research. IoT is used in with organ-on-a-chip technology in the early phases to once again help increase the odds of choosing a winning formulation over less favorable ones and help reduce the development cost.

The virtual organs, cells on a chip, and digital twins that are at the core of in silica research are "smart" and all interconnected via IoT.

IoT also helps with that other often identified problem in clinical trials—patient monitoring. IoT better ensures the success of clinical trials by tracking the health of subjects in their normal environment outside of the research centers where the treatment under evaluation traditionally gets administered. Not only does it lift the obligation for frequent check-ins, but it also broadens the pool of eligible individuals to those who may not have the ability to travel great distances.

IoT is bringing a new dynamic to the pharma industry, one that is already helping to reduce drug discovery and development costs and accelerating the speed of producing new drugs for diseases in need of novel therapeutics.

This aspect of connectivity, drug discovery, and IoT came into play with the rapid development of the Moderna COVID vaccine. As we will discuss in the next section, Moderna leveraged all of what we have been discussing to help bring their COVID vaccine to market safely in record time. Of the many aspects of AI they leveraged was a connected infrastructure—which they as a company had created from the ground up to have everything connected.

As a company, Moderna was not burdened with any old legacy infrastructure, even in terms of their discovery and manufacturing of drugs. All of their lab systems, all of the information systems and devices were already interconnected and talking to each other via the Internet of Things, which meant that they were able to remotely and interconnectedly run every aspect of their vaccine discovery process digitally as well as globally.

AI and the Fight Against COVID-19

Over the course of the past two years, which coincides with the development of this book, we have had an excellent opportunity, for better or worse, to see firsthand how AI can accelerate drug discovery with the real world/real-time development of the COVID-19 vaccines.

In particular, this is the case study of how AI was used to hasten the delivery of the Moderna vaccine. As I said in our introduction and opening chapters, I had the opportunity to sit on a Harvard panel with Moderna CEO Stéphane Bancel, and what impressed on me most that his company "gets it" when it comes to AI is that he described Moderna as a "tech company that just happens to do biology."

As we have discussed in previous chapters, the longest, the most time and resource-consuming aspect of drug discovery is the clinical trial process, and it is in streamlining this process that AI has and is showing the most promise. This is evidenced by the development of the Moderna COVID vaccine, where they and the other pharmaceutical companies involved in the development of the vaccines had no choice but to accelerate the process. It literally was a matter of life and death.

It was Moderna's integrated approach to using AI from early drug discovery through delivery that allowed them to accelerate the entire process and deliver a vaccine not only in record time—the fastest vaccine to be developed and approved by the FDA before this was for the Mumps in 1967, and that took four years—but one based on an entirely novel mRNA platform.

The timelines for the development of the Moderna vaccine are unprecedented and almost unfathomable. What I heard Mr. Bancel say during the conversation at Harvard was that in January of 2020, within two days of obtaining the genetic sequence of the virus from the lab in Wuhan, his team at Moderna had already had the basic design of the vaccine, and after that, it was only a mere four weeks that they were able to send it over to the NIH in D.C. for the start of clinical trials, which were then completed in less than two months.

Overall, there was a huge order of magnitude increase in speed and efficiency across the development process for the Moderna vaccine, and primarily that was because of how well Moderna, at its core, knew how to use AI.

During a recent podcast,[19] Dave Johnson, chief data and artificial intelligence officer at Moderna, said:

"The whole COVID vaccine development, we're immensely proud of the work that we've done there, and we're immensely proud of the superhuman effort that our people went through to bring it to market so quickly. But a lot of it was built on the core [AI] infrastructure that we already had put in place at Moderna. We didn't build algorithms specifically for COVID; we just put them through the same pipeline of activity that we've been doing. We just turned it as fast as we could. When we think about everything we do at Moderna, we think about this platform capability. We were never going to make *one* drug; that was never the plan. The plan was always to make a whole platform around mRNA because, since it's an information-based product, all you do is change the information encoded in the molecule, and you have a completely different drug. We knew that if you can get one in the market, you can get any number of them to the market. And so all the decisions we made around how we designed the company and how we designed the digital infrastructure was all around this platform notion that we're not going to build this for one thing—we're going to build a solution that services this whole platform."

What Mr. Johnson said is perhaps the more valuable lesson to be taken from how Moderna leveraged AI to accelerate the development of their vaccine. It was not only that they brought a much-needed new vaccine to market in record time, but they also used AI and ML

---

19   MIT Sloan Management Review, "AI and the COVID-19 Vaccine: Moderna's Dave Johnson," sloanreview.mit.edu, accessed March 11, 2022, https://sloanreview.mit.edu/audio/ai-and-the-covid-19-vaccine-modernas-dave-johnson/.

to prove the efficacy of a previously unknown type of vaccine and the mRNA delivery system.

This was truly groundbreaking. AI allowed for the creation of an entirely new type of vaccine. The successful deployment of the Moderna vaccine provided not only a powerful weapon in the fight against COVID-19, it brought to the market a novel and game-changing platform technology in the mRNA delivery system, which can now be used for the rapid deployment and development of other vaccines as other novel viruses rear their heads. As Mr. Bancel described it during our panel discussion, think of mRNA as a smartphone, and you can plug different drugs into that platform, just as you would download new apps into your iPhone. AI-driven discoveries like this that are platform in nature will dramatically change how quickly new therapeutics can get to the public in the future.

Artificial intelligence has already played a large part in the war on COVID, in hastening the drug discovery process, not only by facilitating the selection of potential drug candidates but also in monitoring the pandemic and enabling faster diagnosis of patients.

But the battle continues.

The development of vaccines for the treatment of COVID-19 is paving the way for a return to normalcy, and yet despite the effectiveness of the vaccines, whose development was hastened by AI, the risk of the virus mutating into a vaccine-resistant variant still persists. As a result, the demand for efficacious drugs to treat COVID-19 is still of pressing concern. To this end, scientists continue to identify and repurpose marketed drugs for this new disease. Many of these drugs are currently undergoing clinical trials, and so far, only one has been officially approved by the FDA. Drug repurposing is a much faster route to the clinic than standard drug development of novel molecules; nevertheless, in a pandemic, this process is still not fast enough to halt the spread of the virus. AI can and is changing all of that.

"It is always faster and more desirable to repurpose an already approved existing therapeutic than to have to start from scratch," says Eric Siegel.

AI can go through the literature on existing drugs and existing drug trials and molecular targets in a matter of seconds that would take human researchers with conventional computer searches months. When you can find and repurpose an already FDA-approved drug, you have the opportunity to start almost immediately saving lives. The magic of AI is that there really is no limit to the good ideas that the human mind can come up with; the limitation has always been testing those ideas. Now, in times like the pandemic, you can have doctors, academics, pharmaceutical engineers, etc. all over the world thinking, "Hey, I remember reading somewhere that this drug did this thing to this organ, and maybe it can have value treating COVID or XYZ, and AI can run through those tests very rapidly and decide which ones may be worth further actions."

A Question of Trust

As remarkable as AI has proven to be in accelerating the drug discovery process, as indicated by the successes of Insilico and Moderna, there is the issue of trust. This could especially be seen in the volume of vaccine hesitancy. While many who did not wish to get the COVID vaccines refused to do so for political, religious, or similar reasons, many refused because they simply could not trust something that was developed so much quicker than normal.

As AI becomes more ubiquitous in healthcare, this is bound to be a growing issue. However, as people learn more about AI and what it can do, there will come the realization that AI-driven acceleration not only does not compromise safety but results in better screened, optimally developed, and ultimately safer vaccines and therapeutics.

With the introduction of any new technology, but especially one as esoteric as AI, there is fear and hesitancy on the part of the general public. After all, even when airplanes were first introduced, many people were hesitant to board one out of fear for their safety. But as air travel became more a part of regular society, we have now come to the point in time where getting on a plane is as routine as stepping on the escalator at the mall. So, too, it is becoming and will become with AI.

That acceptance is already happening among younger people in colleges and universities, even at the high school level. This is giving rise to a new generation of computer scientists and engineers who will help to implement and bring about many of the promises of AI in healthcare that we have been talking about. We will meet some of these forward-thinking entrepreneurs in the next chapter as we begin Part II.

Where Is This Taking Us

You might note that the above heading is somewhat different than it has been in our previous chapters. Where it was "Where Can This Take Us," here it is "Where *Is* This Taking Us," because AI is already having a profound and transformative effect on drug discovery.

The successes already demonstrated by companies such as Insilico and Linguamatics that are developing real-world AI solutions—accelerating drug discovery for Moderna, Pfizer, AstraZeneca, Johnson & Johnson, Merck, and a whole host of other biotech companies big and small—are driving huge opportunities and investment in AI for drug discovery.

And it is not just the big guys. Among venture capital firms, venture equity companies, and angel investors, there is a lot of interest in any company, any group, or individual start-up that is working on anything related to AI in drug discovery. The largest capital investment in AI by far in the last few years has gone into the drug discovery space.

For example, in June of 2021, Valo Health announced a merger with Khosla Ventures Acquisition Co., a special purpose acquisition company founded by affiliates of Khosla Ventures, LLC, to create a fully integrated end-to-end, human-centric, AI-driven drug discovery platform that aims to improve the success rates for the discovery, development, and approval of new drugs. Valo anticipates the pro forma cash balance of the combined company will be approximately $750 million before expenses, including existing Valo cash, the gross PIPE proceeds, and the net cash held in KVAC's trust, assuming no redemptions.[20]

This is but one example of the millions of dollars being invested in AI, AI start-ups, and mergers and acquisitions, all involving AI and drug discovery.

In general, there has been a 200 percent increase in first-round early-stage funding for AI start-ups in 2017, to over $9.3 billion in venture capital in 2020. Unprecedented investor interest in AI is the primary agent that has seeded large increases in market value, with qtr. three of 2019 data from the National Venture Capital Association highlighting over $13.5 billion in venture capital being raised across

----

20   Cision PR Newswire, "Valo Health and Khosla Ventures Acquisition Co. to Combine and Create Publicly Traded Company Focused on Transforming the Drug Discovery and Development Process," prnewswire.com, accessed March 11, 2022, https://www.prnewswire.com/news-releases/valo-health-and-khosla-ventures-acquisition-co-to-combine-and-create-publicly-traded-company-focused-on-transforming-the-drug-discovery-and-development-process-301308977.html.

965 AI start-ups in the United States alone.[21]

In fact, right now, many who track such things are comparing AI in general and AI in healthcare specifically to the dot-com bubble of the mid-80s to early 90s. The parallels are easy to be drawn.

We have an accelerating adoption of new and potentially revolutionary technologies, but unlike the dot-coms, this is a bubble that is destined to expand but not necessarily burst. Unlike in the heyday of the dot-coms, where VCs were throwing money almost wildly at anything involving internet technologies, with AI, and particularly AI in drug discovery and the healthcare space, you have much more savvy investors who are looking primarily at proven technologies.

Unlike the "vaporware" companies that led to the bursting of the dot-com bubble, AI companies need to prove that what they can deliver are working and complete products to the market.

That is where companies like ours come into play. We have a specific system and process that allows us to identify those nascent AI ideas that have the best potential and help bring them to proof of concept and eventually, with a little luck and a lot of sweat and perseverance, into the marketplace.

---

21   Waterloo Business Review, "Artificial Intelligence: The Next Dot-Com Bubble?," medium. com, accessed March 11, 2022, https://medium.com/waterloo-business-review/ artificial-intelligence-the-next-dot-com-bubble-1bd3277ab968.

TAKEAWAYS

- AI is already making real-word differences in accelerating the drug discovery process.

- AI was instrumental in the rapid development and safe deployment of the COVID-19 vaccines.

- How AI is changing and will change the nature of drug discovery is perhaps its most important impact on healthcare.

- There is remarkable investment and remarkable opportunity for AI start-ups for solutions related to any aspect of the drug discovery process.

This concludes Part I of this book. In Part II, we will take a closer look at where AI is already being used to improve the delivery of healthcare and the remarkable opportunities that still exist for start-ups in this burgeoning industry.

PART II

Healthcare Start-Ups: The Big Picture

*Anything that could give rise to smarter-than-human intelligence–
in the form of Artificial Intelligence, brain-computer interfaces,
or neuroscience-based human intelligence enhancement–
wins hands down beyond contest as doing the most to
change the world. Nothing else is even in the same league.*

—ELIEZER YUDKOWSKY

CHAPTER 8

Where It's Happening

*Genomics, Artificial Intelligence, and Deep Machine learning
technologies are helping practitioners deliver better diagnosis
and actually freeing up time for patient interaction.*

—FRANS VAN HOUTEN

Artificial Intelligence and machine learning are already having a major impact on healthcare across all of the stakeholders we have discussed.

In hospital administration and hospital operations, AI is already making a major difference in logistics and the allocation of critical resources.

My colleague and good friend Helen Kotchoubey, head of expansion at Thirty Madison, told me over a cup of coffee when I told her I was writing this book:

I fell in love with AI and ML when I saw what it could do for our patients and care team when I was at New York Presbyterian Hospital. I was tasked with improving patient flow at one of our infusion centers. At the time, our patients were experiencing long wait times and the tools staff utilized to coordinate appointments across multiple providers, and services were not very sophisticated. We partnered with an organization that developed a machine learning algorithm to optimize resource scheduling and could recommend the number and length of infusion treatments in each infusion chair to minimize wait times. The algorithm kept learning and improving with time and became a valuable tool that the care and scheduling team could use on a daily basis to manage patient flow. The results were amazing. Without adding any resources, the team was able to reduce the average patient's wait time by close to 40 percent with this AI tool. And as you can imagine, this was extremely beneficial to the patients and their overall experience when treated in the infusion center.

In diagnostics and treatment, AI has been integrated into radiology and many other forms of medical imaging and testing. On the treatment side, we have seen the implementation of "smart medical devices" such as ventilators. And of course, we have seen the greatest strides in how AI is now changing the very nature of pharmaceutical research and drug discovery.

As we stand right now, and looking at the advancement of and investment in AI in healthcare over the last five years, we really are much further along than you might imagine.

According to the latest report from industry tracker Markets and Markets, "the artificial intelligence in healthcare market is projected to grow from $6.9 billion in 2021 to $67.4 billion by 2027, it is expected to grow at a compound annual growth rate (CAGR) of 46.2 percent from 2021 to 2027." [22]

That same report went on to say, "The key factors fueling the growth of the market include market influx of large and complex healthcare datasets, growing need to reduce healthcare costs, improving computing power and declining hardware cost, rising number of partnerships and collaborations among different domains in the healthcare sector, and surging need for improvised healthcare services due to imbalance between health workforce and patients." [23]

From an investment and industry standpoint, it is safe to say that the interest in AI in healthcare is only growing. According to the 2021 Healthcare AI Survey from Gradient Flow, [24] respondents to the survey said they wanted to have Natural Language Processing (NLP) (36 percent), data integration (45 percent), and business intelligence (BI) (33 percent) as the three most widely applied technologies in their businesses by the close of 2021.

One of the major driving forces for "where it is happening now," as mentioned in the market report, is the availability of large complex data sets. This is what is allowing AI in advancement in healthcare to achieve scalability, as opposed to in the beginning years when it was just one proprietary algorithm developed here or there for a specific purpose or project.

---

22   Markets and Markets, "Artificial Intelligence in Healthcare Market by Offering (Hardware, Software, Services), Technology (Machine Learning, NLP, Context-aware Computing, Computer Vision), Application, End-User and Geography—Global Forecast to 2027," marketsandmarkets.com, accessed March 22, 2022, https://www.marketsandmarkets.com/Market-Reports/artificial-intelligence-healthcare-market-54679303.html.

23   Ibid.

24   David Talby, "The Current State of The Healthcare AI Revolution," Forbes, accessed March 22, 2022, https://www.forbes.com/sites/forbestechcouncil/2021/04/28/the-current-state-of-the-healthcare-ai-revolution/?sh=6dec927d2980.

We can see a good example of the impact of scalability and leveraging large data sets in how Google leveraged its "Deep Mind" AI to create the AlphaFold Protein Structure Database.

AlphaFold is an AI system that predicts a protein's 3D structure from its amino acid sequence. AlphaFold is a top-ranked protein structure prediction method by a large margin, producing predictions with high accuracy, many of which are competitive with experimentally determined measurements.

But instead of making researchers purchase the tool or purchase access to the tool, Google partnered with one of Europe's leading laboratories for life sciences, European Bioinformatics Institute (EMBL-EBI), to create the AlphaFold Protein Structure Database and make it "open source" or freely available to the scientific community.

The initial release of the database covers all of the twenty thousand proteins in the human proteome, along with the proteomes of several other biologically significant organisms, from E. coli to yeast and from the fruit fly to the mouse. In the coming months, EMBL-EBI expects to expand the database to cover a large proportion of all the 100 million proteins cataloged in the UniRef90 database.

Healthcare AI Start-Ups and Unicorn Valuations

"Unicorn" is a term used in the venture capital industry to describe a privately held start-up company with a value of over $1 billion. According to the Complete Book of Unicorns, as of March 2022, there are one thousand unicorns around the world. Several of those are in the AI sector, and a good number, specifically start-ups that provide AI solutions for healthcare. Google, Facebook, Instagram, and Airbnb, were all once "unicorns," so these AI unicorns are in good company!

Having a unicorn valuation does not mean that the start-up identified as a unicorn has earned anywhere near that $1 billion mark; in fact, most unicorns may not have even turned any profit at the time of being labeled as such. The designation is generally based on how investors and venture capitalists feel the start-up will grow and develop, so it all comes down to longer-term forecasting and predictability. Which in and of itself is interesting since we are talking AI!

But what this all means is that an AI start-up with a unicorn valuation has nothing to do with the way they perform financially but their potential to generate huge earnings down the line, usually through a large merger or acquisition, and that is what attracts investors to unicorns.

> **But what this all means is that an AI start-up with a unicorn valuation has nothing to do with the way they perform financially but their potential to generate huge earnings down the line, usually through a large merger or acquisition, and that is what attracts investors to unicorns.**

Here are just a few current AI unicorns at the time of writing. Since this is accelerating so quickly, by the time this book is published and you are reading it, there are likely to be several more.

In the fourth quarter of 2021, French-based, Dental Monitoring reached a $1 billion valuation[25] for bringing AI to remote dentistry. Using AI and an oral scanning device attached to a smart-

---

25 CB Insights, Dental Monitoring, cbinsights.com, accessed February 3, 2022, https:// www.cbinsights.com/company/dental-monitoring.

phone, the company lets dentists and orthodontists remotely track over 130 oral conditions.

New York-based SWORD Health also became a unicorn in qtr. four of '21 at a $2 billion[26] valuation for its AI drive telemedicine platform that allows them to remotely provide and track physical therapy for musculoskeletal disorders using computer vision and a smartphone.

Some Successful Real-World Examples

Throughout most of the chapters in this book so far, we discussed a lot about what AI can do for healthcare and where all of this can be going. Last chapter, we started to take a deep dive into start-ups and success-ful businesses such as Insilico Medicine, where AI is already being used and making a major difference in pharma research and drug discovery. Here are a few more real-world examples of AI start-ups and relatively young operations that are not only successful and high-valued but are already fundamentally changing the nature of healthcare.

In June of 2020, Overjet, a start-up focused on using AI to help dentists and insurance companies understand dental scans, announced that it had raised $7.85 million in what it described as seed round funding.

According to Overjet's CEO Wardah Inam,[27] who incidentally holds a PhD in electrical engineering and computer science from MIT, the company raised the funds from Crosslink Capital, which led its round, and E14 Fund, which "only invests in MIT start-ups," Inam said.

---

26   Ibid.

27   Alex Wilhelm, "Overjet raises $7.85M for its dental-focused AI tech," tech-crunch.com, accessed March 22, 2022, https://techcrunch.com/2020/06/02/overjet-raises-7-85m-for-its-dental-focused-ai-tech/.

The MIT-E14 connection is not surprising, given that Overjet has been supported by two different MIT groups. Continuing the Boston-area educational links, the start-up was incubated by the Harvard Innovation Lab. More on university "incubators" for AI start-ups will be discussed in the next section.

In August of that same year, artificial intelligence-driven diagnostics company Digital Diagnostics announced that it had purchased 3Derm Systems. Digital Diagnostics, formerly known as IDX, was one of the first companies to obtain FDA approval for its medical device that uses AI to detect diabetic retinopathy without any input from a doctor. With the acquisition, the company is now building out 3Derm's AI system, which detects skin cancer. That was what prompted the name change to Digital Diagnostics, as the company is now hoping to bring AI technology to bear, to be used in the early diagnosis of many more diseases beyond skin cancer and eye issues.

In June of 2021, a start-up called Mendel, which created an AI platform to crunch big data specifically related to medical research, announced it received an additional $18 million in funding to continue its growth and to build out what it describes as a "clinical data marketplace" for people not just to organize, but also to share and exchange that data for research purposes. The infusion of funds came on the heels of what Mendel said in a company press release was "a surge of interest among research and pharmaceutical companies in sourcing better data to gain a better understanding of longer-term patient care and progress, in particular across wider groups of users, not just at a time when it has been more challenging to observe people and run trials, but in light of the understanding that using AI to leverage much bigger data sets can produce better insights."

But, before any of these companies became a reality or grew to the pinnacle of a unicorn valuation, they had to start somewhere.

An AI Start-Up—The Process

There is significant interest in AI in healthcare. There has been, and there is major ongoing investment to the tune of millions of dollars for AI start-ups. You would think then that with the right idea, it should be relatively easy to launch an AI start-up. It is not. Even for the highest-quality, proven algorithm, or AI-driven software, it is a process to go from proof of concept to real-world solution.

It all starts with the idea of incubators and accelerators. Start-up accelerators and incubators are organizations that seek to help start-ups attain success. Start-up accelerators tend to focus on providing start-ups with mentorship, advice, and resources to help the start-ups succeed. These can include "boot camps" or "demo days," where they can focus the attention of the start-up investor community, or other events where the start-ups get to make their pitch to potential investors.

Start-up accelerators and incubators can get involved at all stages of a start-up's development, from the idea stage to proof of concept. However, most tend to focus on relatively early-stage start-ups, as this is when companies can typically benefit from outside help.

An interesting thing about incubators and accelerators in getting a start-up off the ground is something known as the "bump factor." The bump factor is if you have an idea for a start-up and are at a convention or other networking event and "bump" into a trademark attorney or some other relevant accelerator who can help you launch. But, thanks to COVID, such events have been limited, and much of the "bump factor" has moved online. That is where people, and particularly people in AI or other digital start-ups, are "bumping" into their benefactors.

The "bump factor" is basically a euphemism for "connectivity," and as we learned earlier, the Internet of Things is creating a world of greater connectivity, so it is no wonder that an online or digital "bump factor" is playing a major role in the AI start-up process.

Often the "incubation" process takes place in a university where they actually have kind of a global competition for potential start-ups. It is something almost akin to *Shark Tank*, where start-ups will present their business plans as part of the MBA or other post-graduate program. We worked with a medical company that went through that kind of a process at Rice University in Texas.

The company is Forest Devices, Inc. Forest Devices is a Pittsburgh-based medical device start-up company that is developing AlphaStroke. Acting like an EKG for the brain, AlphaStroke uses AI to help first responders and other pre-hospital providers determine if their patients are having a stroke. Stroke is the most debilitating disease in the world, and the mission of Forest Devices is to reduce that disability by getting stroke patients to the treatment they need faster.

In 2017, Forest Devices, Inc. competed in the annual RICE Business Plan Competition (RBPC) and won first place and over $600,000 in cash and prizes.

Forest Devices CEO, Matthew Kesinger, and Director of Operations, Carmelo R. Montalvo, took the stage in front of 400 spectators and judges, delivering the company's presentation at the Jones Graduate School of Business on the campus of Rice University. After two days of nonstop pitching and networking, Forest emerged as the top start-up in the competition, representing the best investment opportunity in the eyes of the nearly 300 judges in attendance. When asked about the experience at RBPC, Kesinger had the following to say: "The Rice Business Plan Competition was an amazing experience, and the investment from our new partners will help us achieve our next milestone."

Today, Forest Devices is well on their way to being standard in EMS care. In 2021, the U.S. Food and Drug Administration (FDA) designated its AlphaStroke technology as a "breakthrough device."

Getting the kind of initial visibility such as at RICE competition is largely responsible for Forest achieving their goals. Getting out in front of the investors with a real working product is vital to any start-up's success and that is what incubators and accelerators can do.

I had the pleasure to speak with Christian Tidona, who runs a similar incubator to the RICE competition, but this one specifically for pharmaceutical research and drug discovery with the Heidelberg University in Germany, where he says it is his mission to "bridge the gap between Pharma and academia."

"Basically, a three-step process," says Christian. The first step—and this is where I spend the greatest amount of my time—is talking with researchers in big pharmaceutical companies and discussing their particular challenges. I help them to ask very big questions in bio-medical research for which currently there is no answer or no good answer, neither in current start-ups nor in academic research groups. Then once we have identified those unmet needs, we enter the second step of the incubation process, where we post these challenges on our crowdsourcing platform worldwide at the best universities and research institutions and invite young academic researchers to solve these problems. Most of the postdoctoral candidates apply by submit-ting a very original project proposal on how to surmount this particu-lar challenge. We usually get between one hundred to two hundred proposals, from sixty to eighty different countries. Of those, we pare down to the fifteen best ones, the fifteen most impressive, and invite them to Heidelberg for a five-day Bootcamp.

Once the finalists have been flown into Heidelberg, they are divided into five groups. Christian says he and his team then mentor each of these groups and help them to develop their ideas into a very solid, very tight business proposal that can be brought to the pharmaceutical companies seeking the solution to the original challenge.

"It's a very intense Bootcamp. The candidates don't sleep a lot. They get a lot of mentorship, and we push them constantly outside their comfort zone. On the last day, they present their pitches in front of 'the jury,' which is usually made up of senior management of the research and development division of the sponsoring pharmaceutical company."

The winner then enters the third phase. "Which is local incubation. So, to recap the process, the first phase is to identify the challenge. The second is global crowdsourcing, and the third is local incubation. We move them with their families wherever they come from, Stanford, MIT, Singapore, wherever they come from, we move them with their families to here to Heidelberg as we all work very hard to bring their idea to proof of concept."

Christian's incubation process and that of Rice University and others at Harvard and MIT, and dozens of other universities worldwide may differ somewhat in their methods, but what it all comes down to is this: every AI start-up is looking for the same three things:

1. Access to customers

2. Access to talent

3. Access to capital

Christian has also recently launched AION labs in Israel, a similar operation to his incubator in Heidelberg, but this one focusing on start-ups using AI for drug discovery. Per Christian, "AION Labs is a first-of-its-kind alliance of global pharma and technology leaders and investors that have come together with one clear mission in mind, to create and adopt gateway AI and computational technologies that will transform the process of drug discovery and development for the betterment of human health."

That is what these university and industry-affiliated incubators and accelerators do and what we do for healthcare AI start-ups at BigRio.

A "Shark Tank" for AI in Healthcare

I like to think that what my company has done is created a kind of *Shark Tank* for AI start-ups in healthcare. If you are familiar with the TV series, then you know that basically, what they do is hyper-accelerated the most important part of the incubation process—visibility. You can't get better visibility than getting in front of celebrity investors and a TV audience of millions of viewers. Many entrepreneurs who have appeared on that program—even those who did not get picked up by the sharks—succeeded because others who were interested in their concepts saw them on the show.

We can do the same. We have the contacts and the expertise not only to weed out the companies that are not ready, as the sharks on the TV show do but also mentor and get those who we feel are ready noticed by the right people in the biomedical community.

We are currently doing this for a company called Alpha Stroke. We are helping them through the FDA approval process of an AI-driven medical device that will be able to evaluate stroke victims in the ambulance and determine how extensive their brain damage is or will be, and then triage them to the best and nearest medical center to deal with their condition.

Where Is This Taking Us?

AI is already changing the patient experience, how clinicians practice medicine, and how the pharmaceutical industry operates. The race to the top of AI in healthcare is well underway.

According to the 2022 AI Index Report, published by the Stanford Institute for Human-Centered Artificial Intelligence, the private investment in AI in 2021 totaled around $93.5 billion—more than double the total private investment in 2020. In 2020, there were four funding rounds worth $500 million or more; in 2021, there were fifteen.[28]

The same report found that AI is becoming more affordable and higher performing. For example, since 2018, the cost to train an image classification system—as is often used in start-ups involving AI and diagnostics or medical imaging—has decreased by 63.6 percent, while training times have improved by 94.4 percent. The trend of lower training cost but faster training time appears across other machine learning task categories such as recommendation, object detection, and language processing.

The report also said that an AI Index analysis of legislative records on AI in twenty-five countries shows that the number of bills containing "artificial intelligence" that were passed into law grew from just one in 2016 to eighteen in 2021. Spain, the United Kingdom, and the United States passed the highest number of AI-related bills in 2021, with each adopting three.

Revenues have also skyrocketed. The International Data Corporation (IDC), a market research company based in Framingham, Massachusetts, predicts that worldwide revenues for the AI market will total $156.5 billion in 2020, an increase of 12.3 percent over 2019. Although growth in 2020 is slower than in previous years due to

---

28   Artificial Intelligence Index, "Measuring trends in Artificial Intelligence," Stanford University, accessed March 23, 2022, https://aiindex.stanford.edu/report/.

the economic impact of the COVID-19 pandemic, the IDC expects that global revenues will surpass $300 billion in 2024.[29]

This all bodes well for more widespread adoption of AI technologies in healthcare.

We have already seen the successful implementation of AI in healthcare. But even the astounding breakthroughs made by Insilco, AlphaFold, and many others are still only barely scratching the surface.

In the next decade, we will likely see an increasingly synergistic relationship develop between biological sciences and AI innovation.

What lies ahead for start-ups in AI for healthcare is a myriad of opportunities for innovation that will advance the health of every human being living on this planet.

This will mean AI evolving beyond making predictions at the molecular level to modeling and simulating the physiology of cells, tissues, and whole organs. As such solutions are incubated, accelerated, and introduced, they will allow us to identify novel therapeutic targets, develop better diagnostic tools and even forecast the unique trajectory from a predisposition to a particular disease or condition through its progression for a specific patient and develop potential treatments or interventions anywhere along that health journey.

In the next decade, we will likely see an increasingly synergistic relationship develop between biological sciences and AI innovation. Biology will inform the design of better-performing AI systems, which will enable extraordinary leaps in our fundamental understanding of health and medicine, which in turn will advance AI research in healthcare even further.

---

29 Neil Savage, "The Race to the Top Among the World's Leaders in Artificial Intelligence," *Nature,* published December 9, 2020, https://www.nature.com/articles/d41586-020-03409-8.

TAKEAWAYS

- AI is here and is already making a difference at almost every touchpoint and for every stakeholder in healthcare.

- There are billions of dollars being invested in the incubation and acceleration of start-ups with healthcare AI solutions.

- Getting from idea to proof of concept to unicorn valuation for an AI start-up is a process that requires guidance and mentorship.

We have discussed machine learning, Natural Language Processing, digital twinning, and how each is changing healthcare delivery worldwide. While each AI technology can contribute significant value alone, the larger potential lies in the synergies generated by using them together across the entire patient journey, from diagnoses to treatment, to ongoing health maintenance.

As hundreds of new healthcare AI providers appear on the market almost daily now, investors face the challenge of identifying the most promising teams to back. That is where BigRio really comes into play and what we will discuss in our concluding chapters.

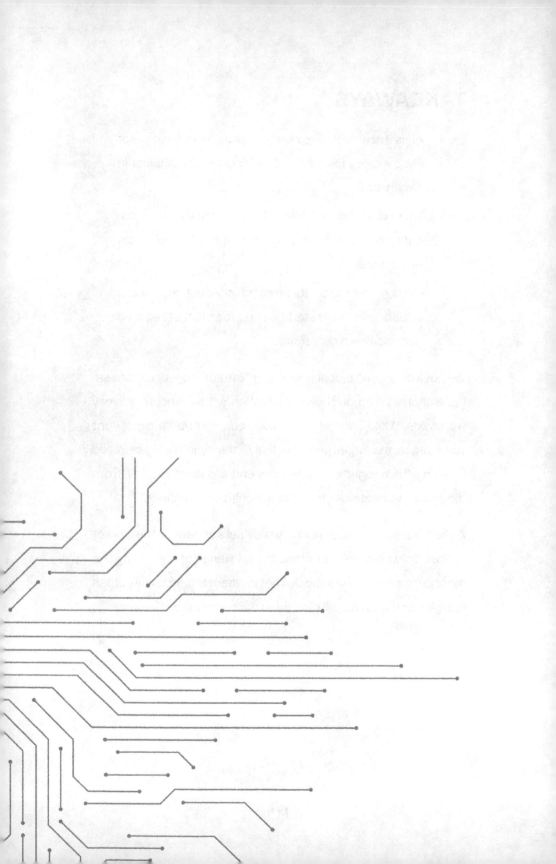

CHAPTER 9

Challenges of Implementation

I believe this artificial intelligence is going to be our partner. If we misuse it, it will be a risk. If we use it right, it can be our partner.

—MASAYOSHI SON

We have spent the bulk of the last eight chapters of this book painting quite the rosy picture of AI in healthcare. Indeed, we are at an amazing time where there is a kind of "harmonic convergence" of all the elements falling into place that are beginning to fulfill the promises of what AI can do to improve healthcare.

However, that is not to say that there are not challenges remaining.

Getting Good Data

As you have come to learn by now, every healthcare-related AI innovation relies on access to very big data sets. The question for any AI start-up is, "where can I get good data?" As discussed in the last chapter, innovations such as Google having made the 3D protein model database publicly available are a major step in solving the data access issue for AI start-ups. However, that is primarily a dataset that is helpful to AI start-ups whose solutions are geared toward medical research and drug discovery.

On the patient care side, most of the data required for AI applications resides in files like electronic medical records (EMRs) and other patient documents, and that creates privacy concerns as a hurdle to overcome before full-scale adoption of patient-centric AI can be implemented.

When it comes to protected health information (PHI), covered entities have a duty under HIPAA to protect patient data. However, as AI technology continues to evolve and healthcare organizations continue to integrate AI into daily processes, gaps in the regulatory space continue to put this technology in a gray area. Are third parties such as AI solution providers subject to all HIPAA regulations? That is a question the answer to which is not entirely clear, but one-way start-ups and AI vendors can get around the issue is to "self-police" and offer their healthcare clients internal

Generally speaking, AI technology is not necessarily any more vulnerable to manipulation by bad actors than any other IT technology.

privacy policies that will make them comfortable and give them iron-clad guarantees about the sharing of any sensitive patient information. This is actually a relatively easy fix for AI start-ups. Since AI developers mostly come from an IT background, they are quite familiar with creating privacy policies for web-based solutions and software service applications.

Generally speaking, AI technology is not necessarily any more vulnerable to manipulation by bad actors than any other IT technology. The same safeguards and privacy policies that have been implemented for other healthcare IT should offer adequate protection for AI-driven solutions.

Even once all of the privacy concerns in accessing patient data for healthcare AI algorithms can be addressed, the issues of data access do not stop there. Privacy concerns aside, healthcare AI-enabled systems require massive volumes of data. AI developers need to know that the collected data is from reliable sources and has been subjected to the bias mitigation techniques discussed in Chapter 6.

Beyond that, in order to use any AI-enabled solution—but particularly ones that are patient-centric—hospitals and healthcare organizations also need to make sure that their collection of data has been "optimized" for AI. That is not so easy for hospitals that are often using legacy data collection software along with newer technologies. A 2018 report on Enterprise AI Adoption found that 96 percent of organizations are hindered because of data-related issues in achieving AI success.[30] To prepare datasets that are optimized for AI implementation, hospitals need to identify the desired outcome at the earliest and prepare data accordingly. Healthcare organizations can also help to bring in AI solutions by trying to ensure that the data is consistent with the processes that the AI algorithm is built for. While AI is very good at drawing conclusions from disparate data sets,

---

30   Databricks "2018 Trend Report: Enterprise AI Adoption," databricks.com, accessed March 23, 2022, https://pages.databricks.com/rs/094-YMS-629/images/DatabricksIDG_eBK0911[1].pdf.

hospitals can improve the implementation process by scrubbing data to minimize missing values and eliminate irrelevant data.

The lack of standardization of the information in EMRs, EHRs, and other patient medical records also presents a problem for data acquisition to AI solution providers. While it has been mandated through Obama-era healthcare legislation that hospitals and health-care facilities implement an EMR system, there was no single system that was required. It has been estimated that as many as half of records are mismatched when data is transferred between healthcare systems. In a 2018 survey by Stanford Medicine in California, 59 percent of clinicians said they felt that their EMR systems needed a complete overhaul. This, however, is a data challenge that is unlikely to change anytime soon. All attempts over the past few years to develop and implement a Standard Health Record, or SHR, have thus been rejected due to the astronomical costs of any such implementation.

Changes to Hearts and Minds

While AI has already made some great strides in improving diagnostics, treatment, and other areas of patient care, when it comes to many physicians, there still is a hesitancy in accepting AI into everyday medicine.

Although AI systems are being warmly embraced by practicing physicians such as radiologists and others involved primarily in medical imaging and advanced diagnostics, there is not a similar level of acceptance among general practitioners.

Although AI-enabled systems at the primary care treatment and diagnosis point of contact are still in their earliest stages, widespread implementation of AI applications in general medicine is still more of a future scenario. Among other reasons that have been identified for the slower adoption of AI for primary care are the general practitioners' lack of trust in and acceptance of AI-enabled systems.

These adoption barriers arise, for instance, from the not-necessarily-accurate concern that AI-enabled systems might be trained with a database that has not been properly screened for inherent biases, leading to inaccurate outcomes. Then there is simply an "old school" distrust on the part of long-term general practitioners (GPs) of technology that seems to be replacing human knowledge and intuition. Finally, there are issues with the implementation of AI systems in the primary care setting, such as a perceived threat to professional autonomy, the aforementioned privacy issues, and potential legal liabilities from using AI-enabled systems.

This is unfortunate because one of the areas that can benefit greatly from what AI can do is primary care. General practitioners serve as the first point of medical contact and, therefore, must diagnose patients who present with disparate symptoms with a high degree of accuracy and proficiency in a very short amount of time.

For instance, a study found that, in Germany, primary care is one of the most frequently used healthcare services, leading to an average physician-patient contact time of 7.6 minutes. Moreover, GPs are responsible for the initial diagnosis, thus setting the direction for whether a patient receives the right care. Misdiagnosis in this early stage of diseases can have a severe impact on medical quality in terms of injuries, avoidable illnesses, hospitalizations, and in 10 percent of cases, death.[31] Besides the potentially tragic individual consequences, such misdiagnoses also can significantly increase the cost of care.

---

31   Christoph Buck, Eileen Doctor, Jasmin Hennrich, Jan Jöhnk, and Torsten Eymann, "General Practitioners' Attitudes Toward Artificial Intelligence-Enabled Systems: Interview Study," *Journal of Medical Internet Research*, 24, no. 1, (2022): e28916, doi: 10.2 196/28916PMID: 35084342.

These are the very concerns that AI can improve or completely overcome for the primary care physician. AI-enabled systems can free up physicians' time so they can spend more time with each patient, or see more patients throughout the day, or have time to concentrate on more specific tasks needed by the individual patient. In this way,

So how do we get over their apprehension? It requires "changing hearts and minds."

rather than distancing the human from the patient, AI will actually enable closer relationships between the GP and his or her patients, as it will allow the physician to spend more facetime with each patient. But most importantly, AI-enabled systems can reduce diagnostic errors, which are considered the greatest threat to patient safety at the primary point of care.

So how do we get over their apprehension? It requires "changing hearts and minds."

"When you are getting a CT scan or an MRI, you do not worry or care about how the machine works or need to understand the minutia of the technology behind it; you just trust your doctor or the regulatory agency that oversees devices that the CT scan or MRI does what it is supposed to do and it will help her or him diagnose and treat you," said my friend Helen Kotchoubey, during our recent brunch.

"I am not saying that patients and doctors, and especially hospital admins who are making decisions about AI implementation, shouldn't be asking questions about AI," Helen continued, "but, it's hard for many of us who are purchasing products or solutions to evaluate the legitimacy of a particular AI solution. It felt like every start-up or vendor who pitched a product or service stated that their solution was AI enabled and would be a silver bullet to solving our healthcare challenges. But those same start-ups and vendors often cite that their actual algorithm is proprietary, and they cannot share details. How can executives and physicians assess what is an effective or a legitimate use of AI? I found that the consultants and vendors who would take the time to explain—in layman's terms—how their solution used AI, how it applied, how it did not apply, were the most valuable partners.

When dealing with some of the companies that have come to us with AI start-up ideas focused on direct patient care, we have found that one of the obstacles they often have had to deal with is that there are still a lot of general care physicians who do not understand this level of technology and the benefits that AI technology can bring to general practice because they are so focused on the "hands-on" medicine of things.

But surmounting that challenge are a growing number of hospitals as in Helen Kotchoubey's experience—that have been able to bridge that gap by having "innovation departments" and people outside of the practicing physicians heading up those departments who can educate the doctors by presenting real-world, practical examples, of how AI systems can improve their practices as well as provide a methodology or framework to assess the AI solution.

TMCx, the incubator affiliated with the Texas Medical Center that we mentioned last chapter, is another example of hospitals and healthcare operations that are bridging the "trust" gap between practicing physicians and the implementation of AI technologies.

When it comes to changing "hearts and minds" of practicing physicians, programs like the one at TMCx and others reflect the importance of having medical doctors participate in the AI design process.

But those kinds of "innovation departments" and hospital-based incubators are still few and far between, which brings us to our next challenge—the development of a winning pitch and business plan.

Healthcare AI Start-Ups Need a Good Business Plan

One of the things that the incubators, as discussed last chapter, have been able to do to help get an AI start-up the capital it needs is helping them to develop their short pitch to investors as well as their detailed business plan.

At the very least, a business plan for any AI start-up should answer the following:

- What problem do you solve for your end-user?

- What added value do you create for your end-users?

- How can you deliver this value?

- How will you make money?

But that goes for any business plan, really. For an AI start-up, it takes a lot more.

With so much competition in the AI space right now, any start-up really has to do something to standout and set themselves apart. So how do you do that?

One way is not only with your tech or your algorithm itself but with your mentors and the members of your team. These are some of the kinds of things that potential investors or adopters of your system will be looking at. Who have your collaborated with in your early stages of development? Did you have a tech advisor? What was his or her background? Are they tied to a major institution like MIT or Stanford or Cal Tech, etc.?

If you can show a strong roadmap from start to finish that connects all of those kinds of dots, then you have a very strong pitch to make to the incubators and accelerators. Once you have made that connection, of course, the next major hurdle is raising capital, but that is exactly what the incubators can help you to do. So, as in most things in life, that "first impression" is so vital.

Beyond a credible business plan, and again this is something that mentors and incubators do, an AI start-up needs to show real-world proof of concept before they can expect a major company to invest in or acquire their solution, or a hospital or other healthcare organization to implement it for that matter.

This cannot be stressed enough. To draw that analogy again back to the 80s and the dotcoms: incubators and venture capitalists today have no interest in throwing time or money at "vaporware," as they did with the dotcoms. They want to see something that works, a practical model of your proof of concept that is real and repeatable.

You can have the absolute greatest idea, the AI concept that will change the world as we know it, but few are willing to go out on a limb on an idea anymore. However, that is where our "shark tank for AI" once again comes into play; we have the resources to foment your idea if our team of professionals thinks it is worth getting behind.

If we believe in you, we can help to facilitate who will collaborate with you, get you access to the data sets you need, help with funding, help you to pull together the right team—in essence, help you to overcome most of the challenges we have been discussing thus far.

But again, to get you to that place, you must demonstrate at least what is called in the industry a minimum viable product or MVP. An MVP is a product with enough features and benefits—even if it is not 100 percent there—to attract early-adopter customers and validate a product idea early in the product development cycle. Eric Ries, who introduced the concept of the minimum viable product as part of his Lean Startup methodology, describes the purpose of an MVP this way: "It is the version of a new product that allows a team to collect the maximum amount of validated learning about customers with the least amount of effort."

Noting Ries's definition and how it related to the "customer experience," this is another area where I see a lot of tech start-ups fall short. They not only have to be able to show that their solution works as an MVP, but they have to be cognizant of who they are pitching it to and not get overly bogged down in technical jargon and codes and operating systems.

A physician or a hospital administrator's eyes are going to glaze over if there is a lot of that in your pitch or business plan. It comes down to two terms that have been around for a long time in program design "UI" and "UX," which are now much more familiar to the laity. The terms stand for "user interface" and "user experience." You need to make sure that any IT solution and especially now AI solutions—since they are so new and "scary" to the potential end-users—have a "simple clickable UI/UX," which means that it is very simple to operate. Even if your app or algorithm is in the earliest stages, it is important to have this kind of "clickable prototype" when presenting your model. Basically, a clickable prototype means that within your prototype or proof of concept model, there are "hot spots" that, when clicked, take you to another page of the design or critical feature of your demo.

Another theme that has often emerged from our discussions with hospitals regarding what they need or want from an AI-enabled application is that hospitals are increasingly looking for platform solutions, not point solutions.

Most healthcare AI start-ups are in the process of developing AI applications that are narrow point solutions. In other words, they focus on one specific disease or on one specific step in a physician's workflow. But in a hospital setting where they have to implement and maintain hundreds of different point applications for various different diseases and workflow elements, these kinds of single-point AI-driven processes quickly become unwieldy. As powerful as your solution may be, a busy hospital may not be able to work with it. Our experience has told us that what hospitals are really looking for are simple, easy-to-use integrated solutions—platforms that connect the dots across systems and departments to orchestrate care around the patient.

Ease of use and the user experience actually brings us into our last and final challenge—training users in the use of the AI solution.

Training Staff and Educating Patients

Another major challenge standing in the way of AI reaching its full potential in healthcare, primarily at the patient care level, is the training of staff and educating patients.

While leveraging AI solutions provides numerous benefits on an organizational, administrative, and patient care level, using them can be complicated. Implementing AI-enabled systems can often require wholesale retraining of staff. Again, this is where "innovation departments" like those described by Helen can help bridge those gaps.

AI implementation in healthcare also will not be successful until most patients are ready to embrace AI-based treatment. Hence, patients also must be aware of AI's potential so that they can trust AI-based treatment. The approach to gaining a patient's trust is a little different than that of a doctor. Patients already have a general trust in medical technologies they may not understand. As Helen pointed out, a patient does not have to know how an MRI works to know that it is an effective tool that their doctors use to diagnose and treat them. It will eventually become the same with AI. But due to a lack of awareness, doctors and hospitals need to start building that trust now by explaining how AI can help them, such as providing a more accurate diagnosis, more precise surgeries, and other ways AI can lead to shorter hospital stays and better outcomes.

AI holds great promise to increase the quality of patient care, but a major hurdle remaining is still that of gaining patients' trust. Changing the hearts and minds of patients is a little harder than doctors. Doctors, at the root of their profession, are scientists and have a greater intrinsic trust in technology than does the average patient.

There is a perception among medical consumers that AI fails to cater to their unique needs and performs worse than comparable human providers. They also feel that they cannot hold AI accountable for mistakes in the same way they could a human practitioner.

A study in *Nature Human Behavior*[32] found that patients are reluctant to rely on AI care providers because they do not believe they objectively understand how AI makes medical decisions; they view its decision-making as a black box. Consumers are also reluctant to utilize medical AI because they erroneously believe they clearly understand how human healthcare providers make their medical decisions.

That finding lends itself to the solution. Patients must be better educated as to how both human doctors and AI both interpret data and make medical decisions. The researchers in this particular study tested that hypothesis by showing the participants two different Google Ads, an AI-driven skin cancer screening application, in their search results. One ad offered no explanation whatsoever, and the other briefly explained in simple terms how the algorithm worked. After a five-day campaign, the ad explaining how the algorithm worked produced far more clicks and a higher click-through rate.

Overcoming the anxieties of health professionals and the mistrust

---

32   Romain Cadario, Chiara Longoni, and Carey K. Morewedge, "Understanding, Explaining, and Utilizing Medical Artificial Intelligence," *Nature Human Behavior*, 5, (2021): 1636-1642, https://doi.org/10.1038/s41562-021-01146-0.

of patients toward medical AI is key to building a largely AI-driven healthcare system. That will only happen when there is a clear understanding that AI only serves to augment the diagnostic and treatment capabilities of healthcare practitioners—and is not and will never be designed to replace them. This will encourage everyone to embrace AI-assisted medical practices.

Overcoming the Challenges

Despite what we mentioned earlier about general practitioners' apprehension to AI adoption, the same cannot be said of other areas in medicine. In fact, a recent study in Korea found that contrary to the perceptions of the general public that AI will completely or partially replace human doctors, medical students, and doctors, in general, are not concerned about job replacement.[33]

In a similar study,[34] researchers conducted a survey of 487 pathologists in fifty-four countries to ask them their thoughts on AI. Overall, the responding physicians showed optimism regarding the integration of AI and, much like in the Korean study, showed little fear of job displacement as a result. Many of the respondents either expressed interest or excitement regarding the ongoing growth of AI in healthcare and felt it would not impact employability. In fact, 42.4 percent of responding doctors felt that bringing AI into medicine would actually create new positions and increase employment.

---

33   Songhee Oh, Jae Heon Kim, Sung-Woo Choi, Hee Jeong Lee, Jungrak Hong, and Soon Hyo Kwon, "Physician Confidence in Artificial Intelligence: An Online Mobile Survey," *Journal of Medical Internet Research*, 21, no. 3 (2019): e12422, https://doi.org/10.2196/12422.

34   Shihab Sarwar, Anglin Dent, Kevin Faust, and et al., "Physician Perspectives on Integration of Artificial Intelligence into Diagnostic Pathology," *NPJ Digital Medicine*, 2, no. 28 (2019), https://doi.org/10.1038/s41746-019-0106-0.

Less than 20 percent of the respondents said they were concerned that AI tools would eventually displace human jobs, and most didn't think the technology would affect their compensation. Regarding timing, a majority of the physicians felt that AI tools would become integrated into diagnostic processes within the next five to ten years.

As for AI's potential impact on "their professional reputation" as a physician, most respondents felt that their colleagues and patients would not view them any differently for using it or that they would actually respect them more for adopting these new tools. However, a small minority (15.6 percent) did feel that the use of AI would have somewhat of a negative impact on how their colleagues viewed them.

Again, addressing the "will AI replace doctors" question: though they are very optimistic about the technology's diagnostic capabilities, 48.3 percent[35] felt that making patient diagnoses should still be done predominantly by the physician. This is again indicative that a good number of physicians do not see AI as a replacement for doctors but as a way to practice better medicine.

This was corroborated in yet another survey,[36] which looked at doctors' feelings toward AI adoption. In this one, a participant wrote, "That is the main aim! To let physicians do what they were trained for—medicine—and alleviate many of the potentially automatic and time-consuming processes they have to face daily." Another participant noted that "AI means less time needed for boring work means more time for challenging work." And yet another participant reflected on his early days in the medical field to make a point about the positive

---

35   Venture Beat, "AI in Health Care Creates Unique Data Challenges," Ven-
      tureBeat, published February 1, 2021, https://venturebeat.com/business/
      ai-in-health-care-creates-unique-data-challenges/.

36   Andreia Martinho, Maarten Kroesen, and Caspar Chorus, "A Healthy Debate: Exploring
      the Views of Medical Doctors on the Ethics of Artificial Intelligence," *Artificial Intel-
      ligence in Medicine*, 121 (2021): 102190, https://doi.org/10.1016/j.artmed.2021.102190.

aspects of automation. "Much like automation for lab tests, AI will free up the providers' hands and minds to focus on higher-order issues. As an intern, I had to spin my own hematocrits at night. I do not miss that at all."

On the patient side, it is still going to be a bit more challenging on the acceptability end. However, because there are so many well-funded start-ups out there, what is likely to happen soon enough is that there will be a breakout company like a Tesla. When you really think about it, Tesla is as much an AI company as it is an auto company. Elon Musk's vision was not so much about designing and building electric vehicles as it was to introduce autonomous vehicles. Autonomy was always Tesla's endgame, and that means AI. Elon Musk is the friendly face of innovation in automobiles that has made artificially intelligent cars palatable to the general public. Someday soon, there will be someone that will do the same for AI in medicine.

> **There will be a remarkable newsworthy event, a significant patient outcome that was driven by AI, and the public will have its aha moment and relax and accept AI in medicine into their lives, as it has Siri and Alexa and dozens of other AI solutions.**

There will be a remarkable newsworthy event, a significant patient outcome that was driven by AI, and the public will have its aha moment and relax and accept AI in medicine into their lives, as it has Siri and Alexa and dozens of other AI solutions.

With "hearts and minds" changing, the biggest problem to large-scale implementation remains digital transformation as it applies to healthcare. Access to data, increased computer power, and increased connectivity are all still the major issues. However, as we covered in earlier chapters, rapid advances in all of these areas are occurring, and it is the convergence of quantum computing, cloud-based solutions, faster connectivity like 5G and the Internet of Things that will eventually bring the full potential of AI in healthcare to fruition.

In the meantime, companies like BigRio are doing all that we can to help the most promising AI start-ups bring their solutions to the table.

TAKEAWAYS

- AI-enabled healthcare solutions are making inroads among all of the stakeholders in the industry. However, challenges remain.

- Opportunity for AI start-ups in healthcare continues to increase exponentially. But, it is more important than ever to have your AI-enabled solution stand out from the pack.

- Changing "hearts and minds" about AI implementation in medicine is starting to happen, more so among providers than patients, but with proper education, patient trust in AI-enabled medical systems is growing.

- The greatest challenges to full-scale AI implementation in healthcare remain technological ones, such as access to good data, connectivity, and computer power.

Every chapter thus far has ended with a heading, *Where Can This Take Us?*

While opportunities abound right now for AI start-ups in healthcare, where indeed will all of this take us? What will the landscape of AI in healthcare look like five, ten, or fifteen years from now?

We will take a gaze into that crystal ball in our concluding chapter.

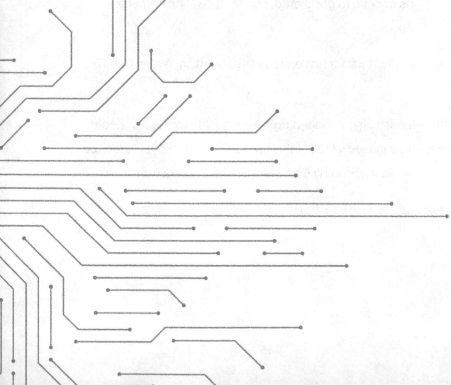

CONCLUSION

What's Next?

Artificial intelligence will reach human levels by around 2029. Follow that out further to, say, 2045; we will have multiplied the intelligence, the human biological machine intelligence of our civilization a billion-fold.

—RAY KURZWEIL

What's next for AI in healthcare?

For start-ups, the future is quite bright. According to a report by Signify Research,[37] published on March 31, 2022, venture capital investment for companies developing medical imaging AI applications

---

37   Sanjay Parekh, "VC Funding for Medical Imaging AI Companies Totals almost $3.5 Billion Since 2015," signifyresearch.net, accessed April 4, 2022, https://www.signifyresearch.net/medical-imaging/vc-funding-for-medical-imaging-ai-companies-totals-almost-3-5-billion-since-2015/.

has totaled almost $3.5 billion since 2015. Despite the COVID-19 global pandemic, the appetite for investors has not abated, and 2021 was the record year with the most funding raised—$815 million. The report went on to say:

1. More than two hundred companies are developing AI solutions for medical imaging.

- The funding raised by medical imaging AI companies is almost $3.5 billion across 290 deals.

- The average size of a funding deal for this period was $12 million, an increase of almost $3 million since the last report.

- Almost 80 percent of total investments raised by medical imaging AI companies is accounted for by the top twenty-five most funded companies.

And that is just in the field of imaging and diagnostics. Overall, the artificial intelligence in the healthcare market is projected to grow from $6.9 billion in 2021 to $67.4 billion by 2027; it is expected to grow at a compound annual growth rate of 46.2 percent from 2021 to 2027.[38]

That report also highlighted some of the most recent notable developments:

- In August 2021, Philips launched two new HealthSuite solutions. HealthSuite solutions allow health systems to integrate informatics applications that can be combined

---

38 Markets and Markets, "Artificial Intelligence in Healthcare Market by Offering (Hardware, Software, Services), Technology (Machine Learning, NLP, Context-aware Computing, Computer Vision), Application, End-User, and Geography–Global Forecast to 2027," marketsandmarkets.com, accessed April 4, 2022, https://www.marketsandmarkets. com/Market-Reports/artificial-intelligence-healthcare-market-54679303.html.

and scaled up or down according to emerging needs. Philips HealthSuite solutions help health systems deliver on the quadruple aim through a connected, protected, future-ready, and cost-predictive single cloud infrastructure and Software-as-a-Service (SaaS) model.

- In May 2021, IBM launched two-nanometer chip technology. It will increase chip performance, increase efficiency, and will help in AI and cloud applications.

- In April 2021, IBM launched advanced storage solutions designed to simplify data accessibility and availability for cloud and AI applications.

- In April 2021, Nvidia announced the launch of A30 and A10 GPUs for enterprise servers.

- In April 2021, Nvidia launched Morpheus to enable cyber-security providers to develop AI solutions that can instantly detect cyber breaches.

Over the past twenty years, there have been remarkable break-throughs in both the fields of medicine and artificial intelligence. We now seem to be poised at a time when the full potential of both fields is about to be realized.

As we enter that new landscape and see the current pack of AI start-ups come online, one thing that is going to be very interesting and very different is that you are going to have companies that are "born digital." In other words, there will be companies that come into this space that are using AI and have always used AI and did not have to adapt any older legacy systems to use it. This goes back to the earlier example of Moderna, who got a jump on the competition in developing their vaccine because they considered themselves a "tech company" first and a "biology" company second. They represented a more "modern" approach to drug discovery and development, then say, a Pfizer or a Lilly that has been around for hundreds of years—after all, it is right there in their name!

As more and more AI start-ups become successful, entities such as Moderna will start to be the rule and not the exception.

Over the course of the next decade, we will continue to surmount the challenges mentioned in the last chapter, particularly as regards computer power and access to data. We are already seeing how computer power is accelerating, particularly in quantum computing. But even conventional computer power typically doubles every few years. Very soon, computing will be powerful enough to enable AI to solve the enormous problems it was designed to do—this is something all of us in AI are very excited about.

> **Very soon, computing will be powerful enough to enable AI to solve the enormous problems it was designed to do—this is something all of us in AI are very excited about.**

Conventional computing in and of itself is getting more powerful. But conventional computing accelerates in a linear fashion. When you add quantum into the mix, it changes everything because it is non-linear. The power of quantum computing progresses algorithmically, which means its processing speeds increase exponentially even as they are applied to solving a given problem—so that seemingly overnight, something that took a conventional computer twenty-four hours to do, a quantum computer does in thirty seconds! This makes quantum computing ideal for bringing AI in healthcare to the next level.

On the data side, thanks to advances in cloud computing, Big Data is becoming less siloed and more publicly available. It is also better data and subject to less bias as bias in AI is being better understood, and improved bias mitigation practices are being employed by AI developers. In addition, while AI is very good at incorporating legacy data, the more we transition away from analog data sources, this will also mean that AI developers will have access not only to more data but better, cleaner data sets.

Then there is the introduction of higher-speed data transmission such as 5G, putting us at a confluence of many technologies, all of which are conducive to rapid advancement and innovation in AI.

Furthermore, as mentioned in the previous chapter, while it may be a bit like turning an oil tanker, hearts and minds are changing as well. In many ways, the COVID pandemic has helped people to gain a greater trust in AI in medicine as more and more patients were forced to accept telemedicine and AI-enabled diagnostics when they could not safely see doctors in person.

The AI Generation

As time goes by, over the next ten to twenty-five years, we are going to see not only companies that have been "born digital" but humans as well! Not that they will be some kind of cyborgs, but we will be raising a generation that will be born into a world where AI is commonplace—even more so than the ubiquity of Siri and Alexa now. If we are now in the Age of Mobile, we will very soon be in the Age of AI, where the Internet of Things will become the "AI of Things." AI tech that is now in its earliest stages, such as fully autonomous vehicles, will be replaced with a time when it will be considered dangerous *not* to hand the steering wheel of your car over to its onboard AI "autopilot."

Just as "Generation I" demonstrated innate acceptance of iPads and smartphones, "Generation AI" will take for granted machines with advanced AI (i.e., machines with minds and an ability to think on their own).

The next generation of humans will be born into a world that will view machines as sentient beings rather than as a cold collection of chips and wires. The philosophical debates about what makes a "true AI" will be a moot point to the AI generation because they will be growing up in a world where machines interact with them in human ways—long before they have any inkling of what distinguishes "artificial" intelligence from intelligence and "humans" from "machines."

Which means that even grade school children will begin to be taught to use the basics of AI and ML, just as they are currently taught conventional computers, and who knows what kinds of innovations kids coming into high school or university with that kind of background and knowledge will be able to create?

The possibilities are mind-boggling on how Generation AI can and will change society overall, but one thing is for sure, it will radically change the way that healthcare is delivered, and medicine is practiced.

The Realization of Completely Individualized Medicine

In short order, the convergence of the most advanced breakthroughs in biology, such as the mapping of the human genome and AI, will eventually usher in a new era of truly individualized medicine.

Once it is fully integrated into the healthcare system, AI will create a new paradigm of "precision medicine." Generally speaking,

AI is expected to help realize the promise of precision medicine in three major areas:

- Disease prevention

- Personalized diagnosis

- Personalized treatment

There is little doubt that AI technologies, when applied fairly and robustly, will open new doors not only for precision but for personalized healthcare worldwide.

The driving force of personalized medicine is that which makes us all unique individuals: our DNA. Combing AI with advances in genetics will make precision medicine even further.

CRISPR technology is a powerful new technique for genetic editing that, for all intents and purposes, allows humans to intervene in evolution. It is a remarkable technology that is already changing medicine and the treatment of genetic defects in incredible ways. When CRISPR is combined with AI, it will make the gene-editing even more accurate and revolutionary.

Much of the controversy and fear, if you will, of CRISPR is the possibility of creating "Frankenstein"-like monstrous mutations either by design or error. The problem, in a nutshell, is that after the CRISPR editing tool cuts double-stranded DNA, the DNA repairs itself but sometimes introduces mutations during the process. Scientists believe the errors depend on several factors, including the targeted sequence and the guide RNA (gRNA), but they also seem to follow a reproducible pattern, and we know that AI is very good at predicting outcomes based on data-driven patterns.

AI is making and will make CRISPR safer. Not too many years from now, a likely scenario will be that a routine medical exam will involve a DNA test. That DNA test is run through an AI algorithm that totally analyzes your genetic predilection toward dementia, or high blood pressure, or heart disease, etc., and instead of writing you a prescription, your doctor schedules you for a CRISPR procedure that snips out those genetic predispositions!

The Promise and the Reality

With the introduction of any truly breakthrough technology comes the promise and the reality. Sometimes, as after the first moon landing, the promise falls short of the reality, and here, fifty some-odd years later, we have not even returned to the lunar surface, let alone "colonized the solar system."

On the other hand, there are times when the reality of a game-changing technology far exceeds even our wildest expectations, such as has happened with the internet. AI in healthcare will be far more of the latter than the former.

Applying machine learning and AI algorithms to large biological datasets such as DNA-encoded libraries is presently shedding light on cause-and-effect relationships underlying human genetics and disease and is already yielding remarkable breakthroughs in drug discovery.

Virtual organs are already taking diagnostics and treatment in astonishing new directions. As I write this final chapter, a press release from the Harvard Medical School[39] hit my inbox, announc-

---

39   Haley Bridger, "Heart-Saving AI: An artificial intelligence system shows promise in identifying signs of heart transplant rejection," hms.harvard.edu, accessed April 4, 2022, https://hms.harvard.edu/news/heart-saving-ai?utm_source=linkedin&utm_medium=social&utm_campaign=hms-linkedin-general

ing that investigators at Brigham and Women's Hospital created an artificial intelligence system called cardiac rejection assessment neural estimator (CRANE) that can help detect rejection and estimate its severity. According to the release, in a pilot study, the team evaluated CRANE's performance on heart-tissue samples provided by patients from three different countries, finding that it could help cardiac experts more accurately diagnose potential organ rejection. That is just one example of the multitude of innovative medical AI models that are being approved for use with increasing regularity.

Moving forward, the exponential increase in biological data generation, advances in quantum computing power, and AI model performance will only accelerate the pace of discovery and further deepen our understanding of biological systems.

This all means not only increased opportunities for AI start-ups in healthcare and medicine on a grand scale, but on an even more profound note, it means bringing better health and longevity to the entirety of the human species.

AI will fundamentally create a shift from reactive to almost entirely proactive medicine.

For almost the whole of the era of modern medicine, healthcare has been reactive. You get sick; you get diagnosed; you get treated. AI will fundamentally create a shift from reactive to almost entirely proactive medicine. As AI delivers on the promise of genetically identical cognitive digital twins of each one of us, such a breakthrough—which is coming—will one day enable us to identify patient-specific therapeutic targets, develop better diagnostic tools, and even forecast the unique trajectory of health from pre-disease to disease and its progression for a specific patient.

Ten years out from now, if we could peer into the year 2032:

- AI will access multiple sources of very large biological and molecular data, which will reveal patterns in disease that will enable remarkable advances in treatment and care.

- Take "telehealth" to its next logical step to true "hospital-at-home" care. With AI and CDT and other "virtual patient" technologies, all but the most intensive surgeries and acute or emergency care that was once done in hospitals will be done in the patient's home. This includes procedures and treatments such as chemotherapy, x-rays, and even childbirth.

- Healthcare systems will be able to predict an individual's risk of certain diseases and suggest preventative measures. This will also lead to a significant lowering of costs for health insurance and for healthcare overall.

- AI will help reduce waiting times for patients and improve efficiency in hospitals and health systems, freeing up doctors, researchers, and administrators to focus on even further innovation.

The AI-enabled hospital of 2032 no longer is one big building that covers a broad range of diseases; instead, it focuses care on the acutely ill and highly complex procedures, while less urgent cases are monitored and treated via smaller hubs and spokes, such as retail clinics, same-day surgery centers, and even people's homes all inter-connected by the "AI of Things."

In the year 2032, AI-driven healthcare networks will be reducing wait times, streamlining clinical workflows, and virtually eliminating the kinds of burdensome administrative tasks that currently bog down the delivery of care at almost every touchpoint. In the decade ahead, the more that AI is used in clinical practice, the more clinicians are going to trust it to augment their diagnostic and treatment skills.

Over the past decade, there has been remarkable innovation in biology and AI, but until very recently, that has occurred largely in separate spheres. As we have seen with the millions of dollars currently being invested in AI start-ups and projected to explode over the next ten to fifteen years, we are now at the earliest stages of a growing synchronicity between advancements in AI and medicine. As AI allows access to large and increasingly accurate and unbiased biological datasets, this will only lead to the design and development of better-performing AI systems, which in turn will enable extraordinary leaps in our fundamental understanding of biology and human anatomy at the molecular level. This symbiosis will continue to drive a mutually reinforcing convergence of innovation in biology and AI.

What Truly Is Next?

Arguably the greatest opportunity for innovation in AI and the greatest challenge remaining is what has always been the holy grail of AI since Alan Turing first asked the question, "Can machines think?"

Even the top scientists and engineers among AI researchers have yet to successfully mimic or fully leverage a human being's ability to continuously learn and transfer learning from one context to another. Neither have they been able to encode our unique capacity to learn new concepts without having clean, accurate, and unbiased data, which is a consistent challenge for most AI systems.

The ultimate promise of AI is to create a digital "neuro-net" that can completely emulate human creativity and imagination to tackle massive scientific problems and challenges that heretofore have been impossible to solve.

Who knows where that can lead? Perhaps to the eradication of all disease or the elimination of death itself. And maybe those solutions are incubating within the mind of an AI researcher seeking funding even now!

ABOUT THE AUTHOR

Rohit is an experienced entrepreneur and leader with a demonstrated history of working in the information technology and software industries. He has been providing innovative data and analytics solutions and products to clients in digital health, healthcare, financial services, retail, automotive, manufacturing, and other industry segments. He is skilled in business and IT strategy, M&A, sales and marketing, and global delivery. He holds a bachelor's degree in electronics and communications engineering and is a Wharton School Fellow and a graduate from the Harvard Business School. He is the President at Citadel Discovery, advisor at CarTwin, managing partner at C2R Tech, and founder at BetterLungs.

Rohit is currently a managing partner with BigRio, a technology consulting firm empowering data to drive innovation and advanced analytics. BigRio specializes in machine learning, big data, Natural Language Processing, and custom software strategy, analysis, architecture, and implementation solutions and also serves as an incubator for AI start-ups leveraging these types of solutions.

With thirty years of experience in IT, Rohit has had a front-row seat to the emergence of AI technologies and has been at the forefront of realizing its many applications in improving healthcare. Known for his thorough grasp over the various nuances of the AI world and his incisive comments on the latest cutting-edge technologies, Rohit is regularly invited to conferences and conventions to deliver speeches and take part in discussions.

He is a TiE Boston Charter Member and also an active angel investor. He has been the Treasurer at the Diversity Alliance for Science nonprofit organization and has served on their Board.

Printed in the USA
CPSIA information can be obtained
at www.ICGtesting.com
JSHW020017290124
56160JS00017B/85

9 781642 255546